# Biking

## ON BIKE TRAILS BETWEEN

## Chicago

BY PETER
BLOMMER

## Milwaukee

# Biking

ON BIKE TRAILS BETWEEN

## Chicago

&

## Milwaukee

BY PETER
BLOMMER

# Contents

## Milwaukee to Chicago (South) . . . . . . . . . . . . . . . . . . . .86

# Introduction

My wife, Sally, and I have ridden our bikes in over 50 countries in North and South America, Europe, Africa, Asia and a number of islands in between. We had travelled for all our lives, but we had grown tired of the vicissitudes of public transportation and the isolation of the automobile. We started biking about 1980 and have travelled only with our bikes since.

In the summer of 1997, since we had exhausted our supply of the better bike routes around Milwaukee, our hometown, we rode our bikes to Chicago, feeling our way along and asking directions and recommendations as we went. We were surprised to discover a route that took us on a series of bike paths, which we struggled to interconnect. After a number of trips between Chicago and Milwaukee, we felt that we had put together the best way to connect the bike paths we had found. Our intention was to avoid traffic and pass by the most interesting places but continue to progress directly to our destination.

We found out that few cyclists realized that they could pedal out on their local bike paths and find their way to Chicago or Milwaukee with relative tranquility. So now I've become a guidebook writer, and I start with the last and nearest route of my bicycle experience.

# *Highlights*

The route from Chicago to Milwaukee is 95.8 miles. Because of a different route on the Chicago streets section, the route from Milwaukee to Chicago is 95.9 miles. This guide takes you the best way possible, but there are varying enjoyment levels because of the diversity of the routes. This diversity leads to unequal distances in the different sections, but each section is integral in the type of riding. These sections vary from quiet paths to somewhat busy streets. The long, good sections far outweigh the short, poor sections.

## The highlights are:
* **Lake Front Bike Path in Chicago** (pages 11 and 152)
* **Oak Leaf Bike Path in Milwaukee** (pages 72 and 92)
* **Bike paths in Evanston and Northwestern University** (pages 20 and 144)
* **Bike route on the Lake Front in Kenosha** (pages 53 and 111)
* **Lake Shore Bike Path South** (pages 26 and 137)
* **Lake Shore Bike Path North** (pages 36 and 130)

## The sections that are good but not great:
* **Racine, Downtown Route** (pages 61 and 104)
* **Evanston, the Street Route** (pages 20 and 144)
* **Kenosha County/Racine County Bike Path** (pages 58 and 108)
* **Lake County Bike Path North** (pages 47 and 119)
* **Kenosha County Bike Path South** (pages 50 and 116)
* **Chicago Street Connection** (pages 16 and 149)

## And, finally, the lowlights. These are usually short:
* **North Racine to Oak Creek** (pages 69 and 96)
* **Highwood Connector Route** (pages 33 and 134)
* **Racine, Direct Route** (pages 61 and 104)
* **Lake County Bike Path South** (pages 39 and 125)

# Chicago to Milwaukee (North)

## Overview

1. **LAKE FRONT BIKE PATH  9.1 miles**
   Starting at Loop along the lakefront on bike path.

2. **CHICAGO STREET CONNECTION  3.3 miles**
   On city streets to connect lakefront path and route through Evanston.

3. **EVANSTON  5.3 miles**
   Chicago border to Northwestern University bike paths to street route to Wilmette.

4. **LAKE SHORE BIKE PATH SOUTH  11.1 miles**
   Sporadic path and connector routes through the north suburbs.

5. **HIGHWOOD CONNECTOR ROUTE  1.5 miles**
   North Shore path does not run through Highwood.

6. **NORTH SHORE BIKE PATH NORTH  6.3 miles**
   End of path north of Highwood to Great Lakes Naval Station.

7. **LAKE COUNTY BIKE PATH SOUTH  9.7 miles**
   From Great Lakes Naval Station to Zion.

### 8. ZION BIKE PATH  1.5 miles
Connects the south and north county bike paths.

### 9. LAKE COUNTY BIKE PATH NORTH  2.5 miles
County path to the Illinois/Wisconsin state line.

### 10. KENOSHA COUNTY BIKE PATH SOUTH  3.5 miles
State line to south side of the City of Kenosha.

### 11. KENOSHA
a) Direct Route 4.5 miles.
b) Downtown Route 8.4 miles.

### 12. KENOSHA COUNTY/RACINE COUNTY BIKE PATH  7.1 miles
The two county paths connect.

### 13. RACINE
a) Direct Route 4.2 miles.
b) Downtown Route 6.3 miles.

### 14. NORTH RACINE BIKE PATH  5.8 miles
Crushed gravel county-maintained bike path.

### 15. NORTH RACINE TO OAK CREEK  6.9 miles
Connector between Racine County Bike Path and Oak Leaf Bike Path.

### 16. OAK LEAF BIKE PATH  8.8 miles
Grant Park (Oak Creek) to South Shore Yacht Club.

### 17. MILWAUKEE  4.7 miles
South Shore Yacht Club on the Oak Leaf Bike Route to Downtown Milwaukee.

### 18. EXCURSION  13.8 miles
a) Milwaukee South Shore Yacht Club to Greenfield Park.

# 1. Lake Front Bike Path

## 9.1 miles

*The best, most dramatic urban bike path in America. The whole path stretches 18.5 miles from 71st Street on the south side to Hollywood Avenue (5700 N). The course is marked and measured and runs through five lakefront parks.*

**ROUTE:** Start at Buckingham Fountain (east of the Loop) and end at Hollywood Avenue. The path runs east of Lake Shore Drive from beginning to end in a north/south direction. At times the path meanders through the parks. There are entrances and exits at all the major streets.

**SURFACE:** Paved. The path is sometimes new, smooth, blacktop and sometimes rougher reconverted city sidewalks.

**TRAFFIC:** No car traffic but bike, rollerblade, jogger and walker traffic can be heavy, especially around Ohio Street and Oak Street beaches and on weekends.

**POINTS OF INTEREST:** Chicago's skyline on the west and the Lake Michigan lakefront on the east. Navy Pier, Buckingham Fountain, Lincoln Park, Grant Park and Montrose Harbor.

**FACILITIES:** Water fountains at intervals. Restrooms in parks. Occasional food stands and at 6.3 miles, the Waveland Cafe.

**SIDE LIGHTS:** Chicago comes to play on the lakefront. You will pass dog beaches, baseball diamonds, basketball courts, soccer fields, volleyball on the beach, touch football and beach action.

**ALTERNATIVES:** City streets on the west side of Lake Shore Drive are not a good alternative.

**OTHER INFORMATION:** The Chicago Park District offers free maps of the full Lake Front Bike Way. Contact:

Chicago Park District
Lakefront Region Office
South Shore Cultural Center
7059 South Shore Drive
Chicago, Illinois 60649
(312) 747-2474

Additional information can be obtained from the Chicagoland Bicycle Federation, (312) 427-3325 (42-PEDAL).

**PARKING:** Multiday parking in parks along the lake is risky. Break-ins are fairly common. You're better off in secured paid lots nearby. Per Kryptonite Lock, Chicago is the bicycle theft capital of the U.S.

**SIDE TRIPS:** Navy Pier Path. Restaurants, bars, etc. 1.3 miles round trip to end through heavy pedestrian traffic. Most likely you will have to walk your bike part of the way. There are no signs that say you can't ride your bike. The road on the north side of the Pier is for auto traffic.

**DIRECTIONS (Mile marker/**Description):

**0.0** Lake Front Bike Path across from Buckingham Fountain North.

**0.4** Chicago Yacht Club at end of Monroe Street.

**0.9** Over the river on separate lane of Lake Shore Drive bridge.

**1.2** Illinois Street, bear right (east) toward Navy Pier just after crossing the river.

**1.3** Lake Shore Path, left (north) well marked.

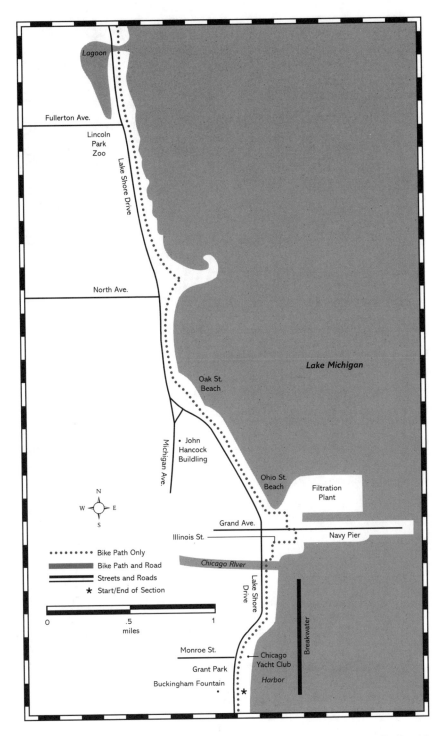

Lagoon

Fullerton Ave.

Lincoln
Park
Zoo

Lake Shore Drive

North Ave.

Lake Michigan

Oak St.
Beach

Michigan Ave.

• John
Hancock
Buildling

Ohio St.
Beach

Filtration
Plant

Grand Ave.

Illinois St.

Navy Pier

Chicago River

Lake Shore Drive

N
W   E
S

•••••••• Bike Path Only
       Bike Path and Road
———— Streets and Roads
★ Start/End of Section

0      .5      1
miles

Breakwater

Monroe St.

Grant Park

Chicago
Yacht Club

Harbor

Buckingham Fountain

★

**1. Lake Front Bike Path**   13

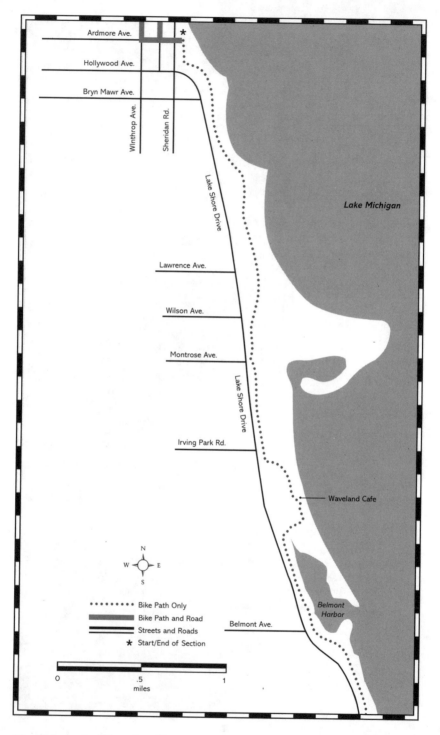

Ardmore Ave.

Hollywood Ave.

Bryn Mawr Ave.

Winthrop Ave.

Sheridan Rd.

Lake Shore Drive

Lake Michigan

Lawrence Ave.

Wilson Ave.

Montrose Ave.

Lake Shore Drive

Irving Park Rd.

Waveland Cafe

N
W   E
S

•••••••• Bike Path Only

Bike Path and Road

Streets and Roads

★ Start/End of Section

Belmont
Harbor

Belmont Ave.

0    .5    1
miles

14   **Chicago to Milwaukee (North)**

**1.4** Left (west) again and follow signs.

**1.5** Ohio Street Beach, bear right (north), curve through park to the water's edge along the breakwater. This is the most heavily used section of the bike path.

**2.0** Opposite the John Hancock Building, which is inland.

**2.4** Oak Street Beach. Plenty of action. Much of interest.

**3.3** North Avenue. There is an exit under Lake Shore Drive. (Most major streets allow an exit from the bike path under Lake Shore Drive.)

**4.3** Fullerton (2400 N.) Lincoln Park Zoo.

**4.7** Bridge over canal.

**5.4** Belmont Avenue (3200 N). Bike path exit is possible.

**5.5** Belmont Harbor stretches for ½ mile.

**6.3** Waveland Cafe. Cute place for food and refreshments; start of golf course.

**6.6** Irving Park Avenue.

**7.2** Montrose Avenue. Path becomes a redesigned sidewalk close to Lake Shore Drive.

**7.5** Wilson Avenue.

**7.7** Lawrence Avenue.

**8.9** Bryn Mawr Avenue.

**9.0** Hollywood Avenue. Lake Shore Drive joins Sheridan Road and the parks end. End of the path after 1 block on the lake side of the high-rise buildings.

**9.1** Ardmore Avenue, left (west) on sidewalk on south side of the street to Sheridan Road. Follow the bike route signs.

# 2. Chicago Street Connection

## 3.3 miles

*A marked, recommended bike route from the end of the Lake Front Bike Path to the lakefront in Evanston. All on city streets. Serious gaps in signage for the bike route.*

**ROUTE:** Start at the corner of Ardmore Avenue and Sheridan Road. The route on the city streets runs west of Sheridan Road except just before Evanston.

**SURFACE:** City streets. Sometimes rough, sometimes smooth.

**TRAFFIC:** Moderate traffic except on major streets. Parked cars on both sides of the street. The one-way streets are narrow, but traffic is moderate and has room to pass you.

**POINTS OF INTEREST:** Urban residential area and shopping districts.

**FACILITIES:** Many restaurants and stores on Granville Avenue and Devon Avenue.

**SIDE LIGHTS:** The Heartland Cafe at Lunt and Glenwood has good food (including breakfast) and the colorful counterculture attitude of the '60s and Berkeley.

**ALTERNATIVES:** Sheridan Road would be the most direct, but the traffic is intense and the lanes are narrow. Just south of Evanston it is illegal to bicycle on Sheridan Road.

**OTHER INFORMATION:** My only recommendation is a good street map of Chicago. These can be obtained at any gas station in Chicago.

**PARKING:** Parking on this route section would be on the street, hard to find and not always secure, especially for multiple days.

**SIDE TRIPS:** Limitless on Chicago streets but none of any real interest on a bike.

**DIRECTIONS (Mile marker/**Description):

**0.0** Ardmore Avenue (5800 N) at end of bike path. West 1 block.

**0.0** Cross Sheridan Road (going west) inland on Ardmore Avenue, use bike lane on one-way street.

**0.1** Kenmore Avenue, right (north). One-way street. Bike route is marked. Parked cars on both sides of street. One lane of traffic.

**0.6** Granville Avenue (6200 N), left (west) bigger street.

**0.7** Go under the EL Tracks and then pass Broadway Avenue (1200 W); all facilities, stores, etc.

**0.9** Lakewood Avenue.

**1.1** Glenwood Avenue, right (north); 2-way street. Moderate traffic, residential area.

**1.3** Devon Avenue.

**1.8** Pratt Boulevard, left (west). Bike route signs are not marking this section. 1 ½ blocks.

**1.9** Greenview Avenue, right (north), no signs.

**2.2** Lunt Avenue. The Heartland Cafe is one block east off the bike route. Lunt is one way going west, so you have to use the sidewalk.

**2.4** Touhy Avenue, then under EL Tracks.

**2.9** Howard Street at Greenview and...

**2.9** Rogers Avenue, right (east) at a diagonal.

**3.0** Sheridan Road. Even though the bike route signs direct you onto Sheridan Road, I recommend continuing east on Rogers for 1 more block.

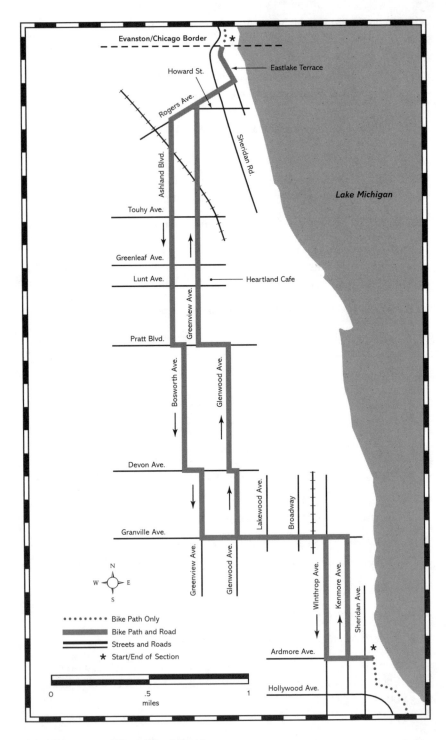

Evanston/Chicago Border

★

Howard St.

Eastlake Terrace

Rogers Ave.

Sheridan Rd.

Ashland Blvd.

*Lake Michigan*

Touhy Ave.

Greenleaf Ave.

Lunt Ave.

Heartland Cafe

Greenview Ave.

Pratt Blvd.

Bosworth Ave.

Glenwood Ave.

Devon Ave.

Granville Ave.

Lakewood Ave.

Broadway

Greenview Ave.

Glenwood Ave.

Winthrop Ave.

Kenmore Ave.

Sheridan Ave.

N
W ◇ E
S

•••••••••• Bike Path Only
Bike Path and Road
Streets and Roads
★ Start/End of Section

Ardmore Ave.

★

0            .5            1
miles

Hollywood Ave.

**3.1** Eastlake Terrace, left (north). One-way street going south. You can use the sidewalk.

**3.2** Sheridan Road (which has swung east), right (east) on sidewalk. Sheridan Road swings north.

**3.3** Enter Evanston. Leave Rogers Park, Calvary Cemetery.

# 3. Evanston

## 5.3 miles

*There is a good route through Evanston. This route follows a recommended route taken from the excellent Evanston Bikeways Map. It is generally on quiet streets and interconnects with the bike paths through the Northwestern University Campus. This route takes you from the City of Chicago at Lake Michigan to Wilmette.*

**ROUTE:** Starting from the Chicago/Evanston boundary on the lakefront. The route is a combination of bike paths and city streets. This section ends at the boundary of Wilmette and Evanston at Isabella Street and Poplar Drive.

**SURFACE:** The bike paths through Northwestern University campus are paved. If chosen, some of the bike paths south of the campus are gravel but most are asphalt. After the campus, the route is on city streets.

**TRAFFIC:** On nice days, the nonvehicular traffic on the bike paths can be heavy. The on-road portion of the route is on quiet to moderately trafficked roads.

**POINTS OF INTEREST:** The Northwestern University Campus on Lake Michigan. There are various routes through the campus, with the ones farthest east affording exciting views of the Chicago Loop along the lake looking back.

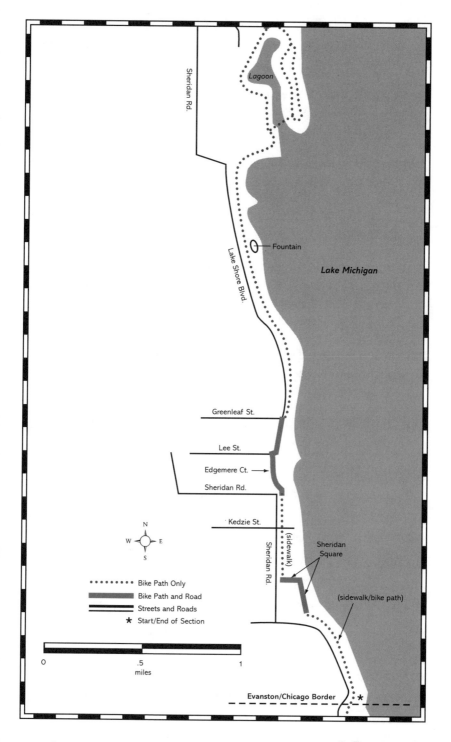

Sheridan Rd.

*Lagoon*

Lake Shore Blvd.

Fountain

*Lake Michigan*

Greenleaf St.

Lee St.

Edgemere Ct.

Sheridan Rd.

Kedzie St.

(sidewalk)

Sheridan
Square

Sheridan Rd.

(sidewalk/bike path)

N
W — E
S

•••••••• Bike Path Only
▬▬▬▬ Bike Path and Road
▬▬▬▬ Streets and Roads
★ Start/End of Section

0     .5     1
miles

Evanston/Chicago Border ★

**FACILITIES:** This particular route doesn't pass any stores or restaurants. There are drinking fountains and bathrooms in the City of Evanston parks at the lakefront.

**SIDE LIGHTS:** The Northwestern University fields and Ryan Stadium. If timed right, on a Saturday afternoon in the fall, you can avoid the hassles of driving and parking and catch a Wildcat football game.

**ALTERNATIVES:** There are numerous options on the streets of Evanston. Armed with the Evanston Bikeways Map, you can find your way north. One option would be if you entered Evanston from Chicago on Asbury Avenue. You can take Asbury Avenue north, but you will have to work your way north and west in north Evanston.

**OTHER INFORMATION:** The Evanston Bikeways Map is distributed by Evanston bike shops, the Evanston Police Department and the Evanston Civic Center. The City of Evanston City Clerk sent a map by mail. The telephone number is (847) 328-2100.

**PARKING:** Good multiday parking on the Northwestern University Campus on the weekends. Otherwise you have a lot of street parking, but with restrictions.

**SIDE TRIPS:** With an Evanston Bikeways Map, you will find there are a number of side trips through the city streets of Evanston.

**DIRECTIONS (Mile marker/**Description):

**0.0** Chicago/Evanston boundary line on sidewalk on east side of Sheridan Road north.

**0.2** Sheridan road swings left (west).

**0.3** Sheridan Square, right (north) on the dirt path, since Sheridan Square is a one-way street going south.

**0.4** Left (west) 1 block on sidewalk.

**0.5** Sheridan Road, right (north). Two-lane road. Restricted parking. Lots of traffic. Sidewalk recommended.

**0.7** Kedzie Street.

**0.8** Straight on sidewalk (north). (Sheridan road swings left.) Through the

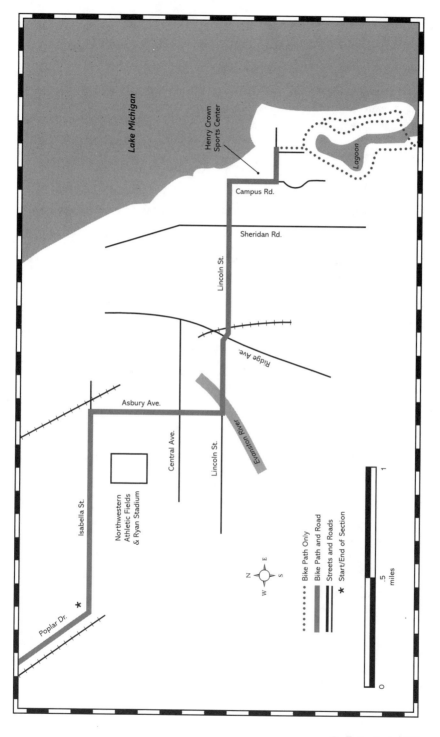

Lake Michigan

Henry Crown Sports Center

Lagoon

Campus Rd.

Sheridan Rd.

Lincoln St.

Ridge Ave.

Asbury Ave.

Central Ave.

Lincoln St.

Evanston River

Isabella St.

Northwestern Athletic Fields & Ryan Stadium

Poplar Dr.

N
W E
S

Bike Path Only
Bike Path and Road
Streets and Roads
★ Start/End of Section

0          .5          1
        miles

**3. Evanston** 23

gate to quiet road (Edgemere Court). Go one block.

**0.9** Right (east) after the gates. Then a quick left (north) on Lake Shore Boulevard (one-way street) along the beach going north one block.

**1.1** Greenleaf Street. Go right (east) on paved bike path through the park toward Northwestern University. Good views back toward Chicago. Continue north on bike path through the park along the lakeshore.

**2.1** Right (east) on bike path onto Northwestern University campus. The bike path swings north along the lakeshore.

**2.4** T junction in bike path. 2 options. Equidistant but looking back on the lake side route are excellent (last chance) vistas of the Chicago Loop.

**OPTION A:** Left along the lagoon on the campus side.

**OPTION B:** Right across the bridge along the lagoon on the lake side. Choice of 2 paths, a) along the lagoon or b) along the lake. Merge, stay left.

**2.8** Merge, 2 paths rejoin.

**2.9** Left (west) toward the campus along the campus road at stop sign.

**3.0** Right (north) on the unmarked road at stop sign.

**3.1** Henry Crown Sports Center.

**3.3** Left (west), road swings left. Follow the road.

**3.4** Cross Sheridan Road. Stop light. Lincoln Street west of Sheridan. Follow the bike route signs straight (west). Quiet Street.

**3.8** Under an overpass.

**4.1** Asbury Avenue, right (north). Just over a bridge. There are no signs for the bike route.

**4.2** Central Street.

**4.6** Isabella Street, left (west). No signs for the bike route.

**4.8** Northwestern University Athletic Fields.

**5.3** Poplar Avenue, right (north). There is a sign "To Green Bay Trail". Railroad tracks on your left.

**WARNING:** After entering Wilmette, the route is complicated. If you lose the route, continue to head north on the east side of the Metra railroad tracks. The bike path runs along these tracks on the east side. Eventually you will always find the trail.

# 4. Lake Shore Bike Path South

## 11.1 miles

*This is the longest segment of the full trip. This is one of the sections that inspired this guide since it is very easy to lose the way and involves a lot of connections between sections of off-road bike paths. When you are on the trails you can relax, but in between you have to be conscious of these directions.*

**ROUTE:** This route involves lots of connections between bike paths but generally follows the Metra Railroad tracks. The road that generally runs parallel is Green Bay Road, but this is not always the case. Even the local bike riders are confused in this section. This route starts at the Wilmette/Evanston boundary and ends in Highwood.

**SURFACE:** The bike paths are sometimes paved and other times gravel or dirt. All of the roads and parking lots are paved.

**TRAFFIC:** On the bike trails in some areas the bike, walking or rollerblade traffic can be moderately heavy, especially on the weekends. All the connector roads are pretty quiet. Take care through the parking lots since cars can be backing out of parking places.

**POINTS OF INTEREST:** There are many since you are pedaling through the picturesque North Shore suburbs of Chicago. You pass through Wilmette, Kenilworth, Winnetka, Glencoe, Ravinia and Highland Park. The route goes through all of the business districts.

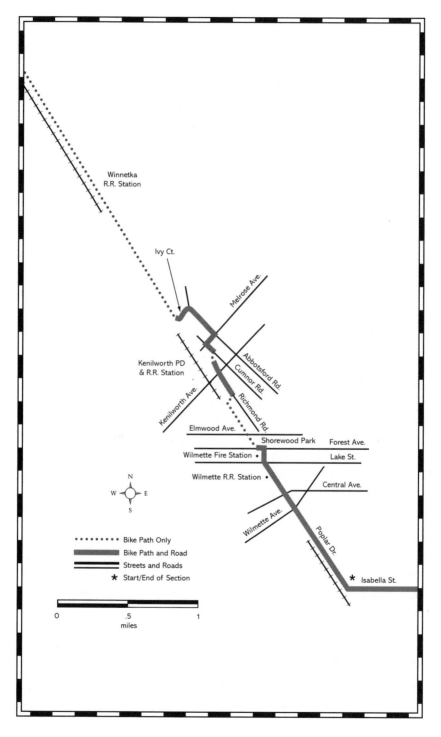

Winnetka
R.R. Station

Ivy Ct.

Melrose Ave.

Kenilworth PD
& R.R. Station

Abbotsford Rd.

Cumnor Rd.

Kenilworth Ave.

Richmond Rd.

Elmwood Ave.

Shorewood Park

Forest Ave.

Wilmette Fire Station •

Lake St.

Wilmette R.R. Station •

Central Ave.

N
W 〜 E
S

Wilmette Ave.

Poplar Dr.

•••••••• Bike Path Only

Bike Path and Road

Streets and Roads

★ Start/End of Section

★ Isabella St.

0          .5          1
miles

**FACILITIES:** There are all types of stores and restaurants in all of these business districts. There is an occasional water fountain in the parks.

**SIDE LIGHTS:** Ravinia Park. This route literally takes you past the main gate. There are concerts (including the Chicago Symphony Orchestra) all summer long in an outside venue.

**ALTERNATIVES:** Using a good local map, you will find street routes available through all these suburbs east of this route. If speed is your intention, you can continue on St. John's Avenue (a busy two-lane road) at County Line Road (7.2 miles) to Laurel Avenue (9.9 miles) instead of getting back onto the bike path.

**OTHER INFORMATION:** A section of *Hiking and Biking in Cook County, Illinois* by Jim Hochgesang describes this route and other interconnected routes in Cook County.

**PARKING:** There is plenty of parking in all the train station parking lots, but be careful of parking limits and restrictions. On weekends, I've had no problems, even for multiday use.

**SIDE TRIPS:** Here is a side trip that you can devote an additional day to: a trip to the Chicago Botanical Garden. From the Botanical Garden at Lake Cook Road in Glencoe, there is a 19.1 mile asphalt bike trail along the Skokie Lagoons and the Chicago River to Caldwell and Devon Avenues on the north side of Chicago. To get to the Botanical Gardens, at County Line Avenue (7.2 miles) go west on the sidewalk on the north side of Lake Cook Road (County Line Avenue is Lake Cook Road toward the west). It is 0.6 miles to the main entrance. Bikes are not allowed on the garden trails, but there are bike racks near the entrance.

**DIRECTIONS (Mile marker/**Description):

**0.0** Poplar Avenue and Isabella Street, going north on Poplar Avenue.

**0.5** Go straight and cross Wilmette Avenue into a parking lot toward the start of the bike path even though the sign says "No Outlet".

**0.6** Pass the Wilmette train station through the parking lots.

**0.7** Cross Lake Avenue. Sign says "Do not Enter" but you (on a bike) can enter. Pass the fire station.

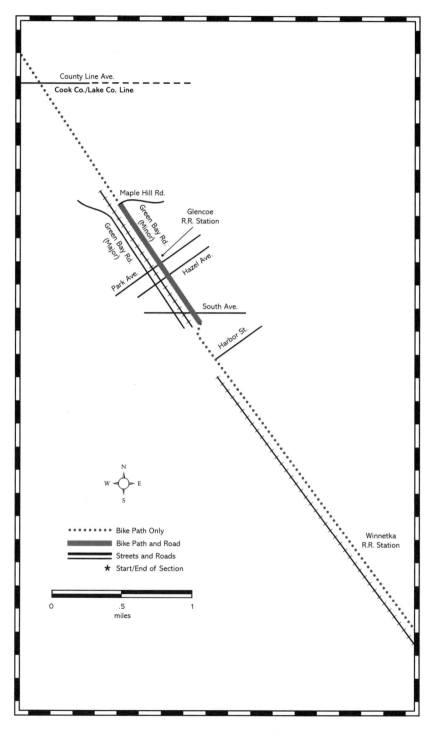

County Line Ave.

**Cook Co./Lake Co. Line**

Maple Hill Rd.

Green Bay Rd. (Minor)

Glencoe R.R. Station

Green Bay Rd. (Major)

Hazel Ave.

Park Ave.

South Ave.

Harbor St.

N
W   E
S

•••••••• Bike Path Only

▨ Bike Path and Road

━━ Streets and Roads

★ Start/End of Section

0      .5      1
miles

Winnetka R.R. Station

**0.9** Forest Avenue, left (west) 100 feet, then a quick right (north) into Shorewood Park on the bike path (narrow, paved).

**1.0** Cross brick road (Elmwood Avenue).

**1.4** Bike path swings right (east) onto short, gravel path to road.

**1.4** Richmond Road, left (north), follow bike route signs. End of trail. Stay on the east side of the railroad tracks going north.

**1.4** Cross Kenilworth Avenue. There is a fountain in the middle of the street. You are now on Richmond Road (north). Pass the railroad station and the police station.

**1.5** Jog right onto a short bike connector trail, which brings you out to Cumnor Road. Left (north) 100 feet. Follow bike route signs.

**1.6** Melrose Avenue, right (east) for 1 block to...

**1.7** Abbotsford Road, left (north), two blocks.

**1.9** Ivy Court, left (west). Follow bike route signs for 1 short block.

**2.0** Bear left (south) up a short hill on a bike path. Follow signs. Paved bike path swings 180 degrees to north along the railroad tracks again.

**3.2** Winnetka Train Station on bike path.

**4.9** Harbor Street. Cross road and turn onto bike path (paved). Stay near the railroad tracks through Shelton park, going north. Glencoe. Stay left on paved bike path.

**5.1** Bike path along the railroad tracks (north); gravel.

**5.3** Straight onto sidewalk (north) for 200 feet.

**5.3** South Avenue. Take Green Bay Road (minor road) north. This road runs east of the railroad tracks and is a quiet road. It is not the Green Bay Road that runs west of the railroad tracks.

**5.5** Pass "No Outlet" sign, north. Pass "Dead End" sign to end of road onto short connector bike path (paved) north.

**5.6** Cross Hazel Avenue onto bike path/sidewalk (north).

**5.7** Cross Park Avenue onto Green Bay Road (straight) north. Glencoe Train Station. Quiet road.

**6.2** Cross Maple Hill Road, straight (north) onto the bike path, gravel.

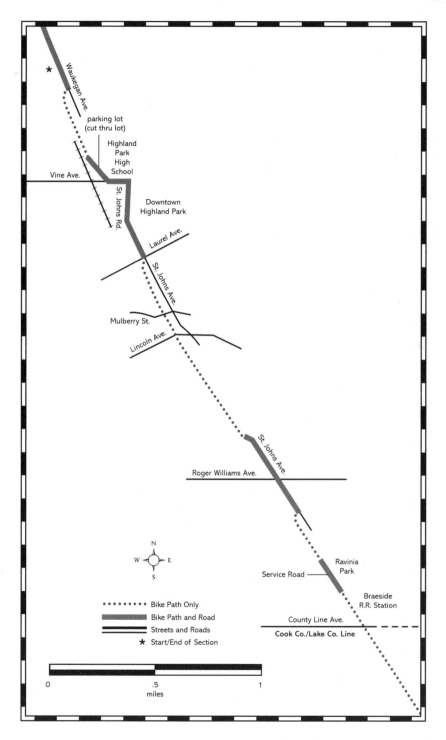

Waukegan Ave.

★

parking lot
(cut thru lot)

Highland
Park
High
School

Vine Ave.

St. Johns Rd.

Downtown
Highland Park

Laurel Ave.

St. Johns Ave.

Mulberry St.

Lincoln Ave.

St. Johns Ave.

Roger Williams Ave.

N
W ◆ E
S

Ravinia
Park

Service Road

Braeside
R.R. Station

••••••••• Bike Path Only
Bike Path and Road
Streets and Roads
★ Start/End of Section

County Line Ave.
**Cook Co./Lake Co. Line**

0        .5        1
miles

**4. Lake Shore Bike Path South   31**

**6.6** Golf course on east.

**7.2** County Line Road; Cook County/Lake County Boundary. Cross and go straight (north) through the parking lot for Braeside train station.

**7.4** Straight (north) through the parking lot to the gravel bike path at the north end.

**7.6** Straight (north). Path ends and joins service road along the railroad toward Ravinia Park.

**7.7** Pass the entrance to Ravinia Park.

**7.9** Straight onto the gravel bike path again (north).

**8.2** Straight. Bike path ends. Take St. John's Avenue. Sidewalk. Parallel road (north).

**8.3** Pass Roger Williams Avenue. Stop sign. Bear left slightly into parking lot to the end and onto the bike path; gravel, north.

**9.3** Cross Lincoln Avenue W.

**9.5** Go over the bridge over Mulberry Street. Path is now paved into the parking lot.

**9.8** Pass through the parking lot for Highland Park Railroad Station to end.

**9.9** Pass Laurel Avenue and go straight (north) onto St. John's Avenue.

**10.0** North on St. John's Avenue through Downtown Highland Park. Two-lane road, moderate traffic.

**10.4** Vine Avenue, left (west). No signs for bike route. 1 ½ blocks.

**10.5** Right (north) into parking lot for Highland Park High School. Cut through parking lot to northwest corner of the lot.

**10.6** Straight (north) on gravel bike path.

**11.1** Waukegan Avenue (parallel road), bear right (north) over curb; two wide lanes, can use sidewalk next to the road.

# 5. Highwood Connector Route

## 1.5 miles

*All of this section is on a busy street. You use this section strictly to connect the bike trails on either side. Sheridan Road is two lanes with some room for bikes but no designated lane. It is possible to ride on a bumpy sidewalk on the east side of the road.*

**ROUTE:** Through Highwood along Sheridan Road straight north. You start on Waukegan Avenue, which becomes Sheridan Road in downtown Highwood.

**SURFACE:** All on highway with a curb.

**TRAFFIC:** This road is heavily used and is consistently the busiest section of the whole bike route.

**POINTS OF INTEREST:** Fort Sheridan is on a beautiful parcel of land along Lake Michigan. It has been closed and should be developed.

**FACILITIES:** Just south of Old Elm Road, there are fast-food restaurants and convenience stores. In downtown Highwood, there are many restaurants.

**SIDE LIGHTS:** Highwood is a military town.

**ALTERNATIVES:** I wish there were some.

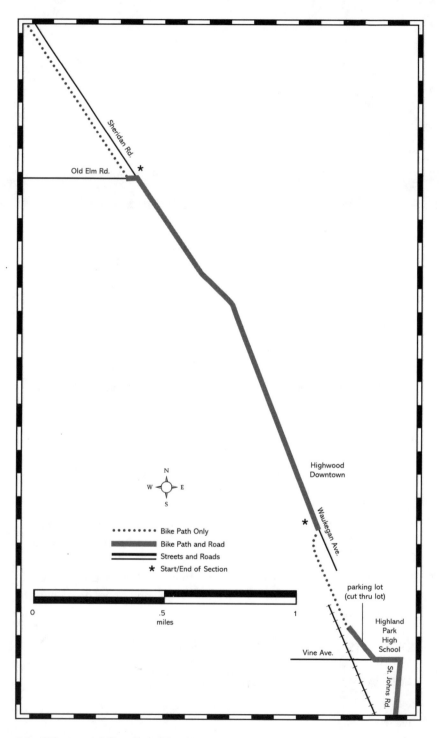

N
W · E
S

· · · · · Bike Path Only

Bike Path and Road

Streets and Roads

★ Start/End of Section

0       .5       1
miles

Sheridan Rd.

Old Elm Rd.

Highwood
Downtown

Waukegan Ave.

parking lot
(cut thru lot)

Highland
Park
High
School

Vine Ave.

St. Johns Rd.

**OTHER INFORMATION:** Really, no other information is necessary.

**PARKING:** Street parking is possible in downtown Highwood but not north of the town on the highway. You could park at the fast food restaurants near Old Elm Road.

**SIDE TRIPS:** None.

**DIRECTIONS (Mile marker/**Description):

**0.0** Waukegan Avenue, north, just south of Downtown Highwood at end of North Shore Bike Trail.

**0.3** Downtown Highwood. Waukegan Avenue becomes Sheridan Road.

**0.6** Start of Ft. Sheridan.

**1.5** Old Elm Road, left (west) for 50 feet then right (north) on bike path (paved) along the railroad tracks.

# 6. North Shore Bike Path North

## *6.3 miles*

*This is the first section of the continuous bike path to Kenosha, Wisconsin. The path starts at Old Elm Road just north of Highwood. The end of this section is opposite Great Lakes Naval Station, 0.6 miles south of the main entrance on Sheridan Road where the path changes from asphalt to cement. This is the point where the North Shore Path becomes the Green Bay Trail. You pass through Lake Bluff and Lake Forest.*

**ROUTE:** Generally, the route runs between the army and the navy, from Fort Sheridan to Great Lakes Naval Station. The off-road path runs alongside Sheridan Road on the east and the Metra Railroad Tracks on the west. In Lake Forest, you pass through the railroad station parking lot, which connects the path north and south. There is a bike route sign in Lake Forest. Don't follow it. Stay north through the railroad station parking lot.

**SURFACE:** This section of the bike path is asphalt. There is a short connector section through the railroad station parking lot in Lake Forest.

**TRAFFIC:** There is moderate bike traffic on this section. There are few crossroads, some crossed by bridges. Take care in the parking lot.

**POINTS OF INTEREST:** The suburban downtown shopping area of Lake Forest and the pleasant Village of Lake Bluff.

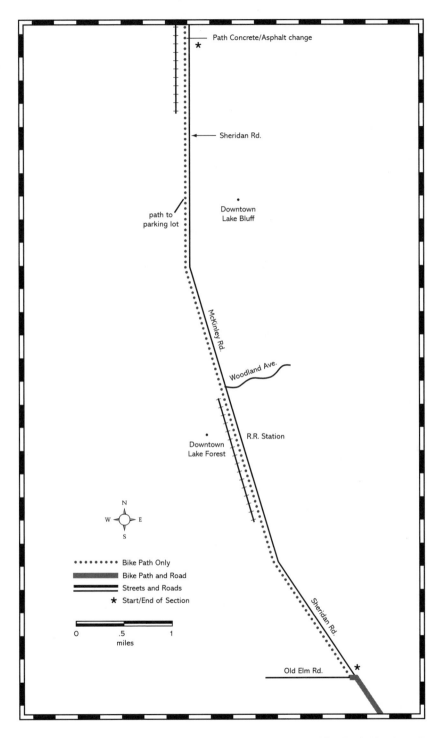

Path Concrete/Asphalt change

Sheridan Rd.

Downtown
Lake Bluff

path to
parking lot

McKinley Rd.

Woodland Ave.

R.R. Station

Downtown
Lake Forest

N
W   E
S

•••••••• Bike Path Only
▬▬▬▬ Bike Path and Road
━━━━ Streets and Roads
★ Start/End of Section

0    .5    1
miles

Sheridan Rd.

Old Elm Rd.

**FACILITIES:** Plenty of restaurants and stores in Lake Forest and Lake Bluff.

**SIDE LIGHTS:** An interesting tour of Lake Forest will show you Chicago's most affluent suburb.

**ALTERNATIVES:** Side roads through Lake Forest and Lake Bluff east of the bike path can be explored. A local map will be needed.

**OTHER INFORMATION:** A section of *Hiking and Biking in Lake County, Illinois* by Jim Hochgesang describes this route and other interconnected routes in Lake County.

**PARKING:** There is good parking in the train station parking lots for Lake Forest, Lake Bluff and Great Lakes. There is no parking lot at Old Elm Road, but there are restaurant parking lots just south on Sheridan Road.

**SIDE TRIPS:** Just wander around east of the trail in Lake Bluff and especially Lake Forest. In Lake Forest, go east to Lake Michigan, where there is a public beach.

**DIRECTIONS (Mile marker/**Description):

**0.0** Sheridan Road and Old Elm Road just north of Highwood. Take Old Elm Road west 50 feet, then right (north) on blacktop bike path.

**0.5** Straight (north); end of Ft. Sheridan.

**2.4** Over the bridge into the parking lot for the Lake Forest Metra Station. Go straight (north) through the parking lot. DO NOT follow "Bike Route" signs for a different bike route through Lake Forest.

**2.6** Lake Forest Railroad Station. Continue through parking lot.

**2.9** Straight (north) out of north end of the parking lot on bike path. Go over bridge at Woodland Avenue.

**4.4** Bear right at Y in bike path. Stay close to the road. Over bridge, straight (north).

**4.6** Downtown Lake Bluff on the right. Food, drinks, etc. Path continues on alongside Sheridan Road.

**6.3** Straight (north). Bike path turns to concrete. This is the North Shore Path of Lake County.

# 7. Lake County Bike Path South

## *9.7 miles*

*This section is all on dedicated bike trail. The trail begins just south of the main entrance to Great Lakes Naval Station just west of Sheridan Road and ends at Carmel Avenue in Zion. This path, called the North Shore Path, was built on the old North Shore Railway right of way and runs north and south straight through Waukegan and North Chicago in Lake County.*

**ROUTE:** Because it follows the old rail right of way, it is straight. Through the urban communities of Waukegan and North Chicago, there are numerous street crossings. The route is adjacent to busy streets for the first 2 miles of this route section. The route directions are complex, but the signage is very good. Under the underpass, watch for broken glass and debris.

**SURFACE:** This section starts where the asphalt path becomes a cement bike/walking path. (Green Bay Trail.) The part along Sheridan Road is paved. The northern part of this section has a well-maintained crushed gravel surface.

**TRAFFIC:** Throughout this section, the bike and walking traffic is light to moderate. Because of the numerous cross streets, however, your progress will be slowed.

**POINTS OF INTEREST:** Great Lakes Naval Training Station, which covers 1,628 acres and trains 30,000 recruits annually, employs over

9,000 military and 3,500 civilian employees.

**FACILITIES:** In spite of being in urban surroundings, there are no water fountains or restrooms. Restaurants and stores are available. At Washington Street there is a bakery.

**SIDE LIGHTS:** None.

**ALTERNATIVES:** City streets are available, especially through Waukegan. Also, depending on your tolerance level for traffic, Highway 32 is a fast, straight alternative.

**OTHER INFORMATION:** A section of *Hiking and Biking in Lake County, Illinois* by Jim Hochgesang describes this route and other interconnected routes in Lake County.

Also, a cartoonlike map of Lake County that does not show the bike path is available from:

The Lake County Convention & Visitors Bureau
401 North Riverside Drive, Suite 5
Gurnee, Illinois 60031-5906
(847) 662-2700 (800) 525-3669 or
FAX (847) 662-2702

**PARKING:** There is plenty of day parking on the streets along this route. A good parking lot for day use and multiple day use is at the train station for Great Lakes near Farragut Avenue on Sheridan Road.

**SIDE TRIPS:** Take Carmel Boulevard east, then east on 32nd Street to Elisha Avenue, south to 33rd Street, east to Sheridan Road, north for ½ block to the corner of Sheridan Road and Carmel Boulevard where the Illinois Beach State Park path commences on the right.

**DIRECTIONS (Mile marker/**Description):
**0.0** Continue north on concrete bike path.

**0.6** Farragut Avenue. Opposite the main gate to Great Lakes Naval Station.

**0.8** 24th Street, right (east); cross Sheridan Road. Follow signs for bike path. Cloverleaf down under an underpass. Bike path is on the north

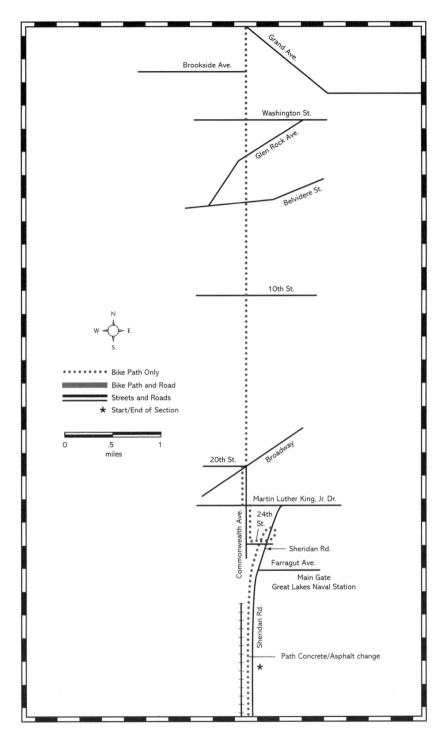

Grand Ave.

Brookside Ave.

Washington St.

Glen Rock Ave.

Belvidere St.

10th St.

N
W — E
S

Bike Path Only
Bike Path and Road
Streets and Roads
★ Start/End of Section

0     .5     1
miles

20th St.

Broadway

Martin Luther King, Jr. Dr.

Commonwealth Ave.

24th
St.

Sheridan Rd.

Farragut Ave.

Main Gate
Great Lakes Naval Station

Sheridan Rd.

Path Concrete/Asphalt change

★

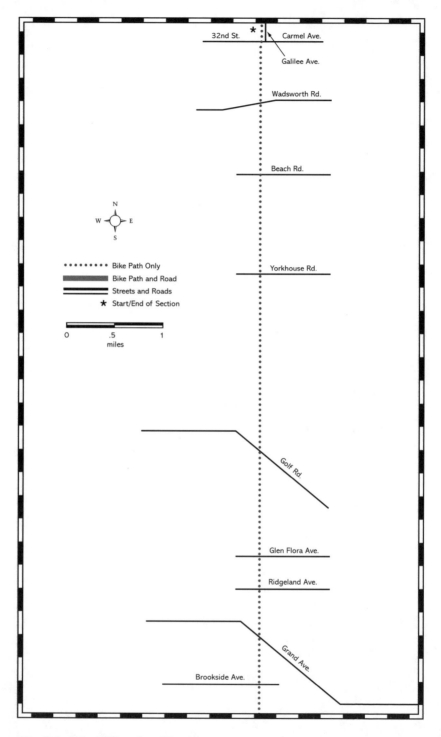

**Chicago to Milwaukee (North)**

side of the road. Watch for broken glass and debris. Possibly avoid potential flats by taking the street under the 2 bridges; on 24th street to the red light.

**1.1** Commonwealth Avenue, bear right (north) on east side on bike path adjacent to the road.

**1.5** Cross over to the other side of Commonwealth Avenue at Martin Luther King, Jr., Drive (stop light). Bike path is now on west side of the street.

**1.6** Cross Broadway Avenue and 20th Street. The bike path is now crushed gravel. Lake County Bike Path going north. Start through North Chicago followed by Waukegan with multiple cross roads.

**2.9** 10th Street.

**3.6** Belvidere Street. Now going west of Waukegan.

**3.9** Glen Rock Avenue.

**4.2** Washington Street (Bakery to right).

**4.5** Brookside Avenue.

**4.9** Grand Avenue.

**5.2** Ridgeland Avenue.

**5.4** Glen Flora Avenue.

**6.3** Golf Road.

**7.7** York House Road.

**8.5** Beach Road.

**9.2** Over bridge at Wadsworth Road.

**9.7** Carmel Avenue. North Shore Bike Path ends and a paved bike path begins on the west side of Galilee Avenue going north through Zion.

# 8. Zion Bike Path

## *1.5 miles*

*This is a connector route between the south and north sections of the Lake County Bike Path.*

**ROUTE:** Carmel Avenue alongside of Galilee Avenue in Zion to 21st Street on a bike path.

**SURFACE:** The off-road bike path is paved.

**TRAFFIC:** Very light bike traffic.

**POINTS OF INTEREST:** None.

**FACILITIES:** A market for food and drinks .9 miles from Carmel Avenue on east side of Galilee Avenue.

**SIDE LIGHTS:** None.

**ALTERNATIVES:** If preferred, you can ride on Galilee Avenue, which has moderate traffic and is wide.

**OTHER INFORMATION:** A section of *Hiking and Biking in Lake County, Illinois* by Jim Hochgesang describes this route and other interconnected routes in Lake County.

**PARKING:** There is street parking along Galilee Avenue.

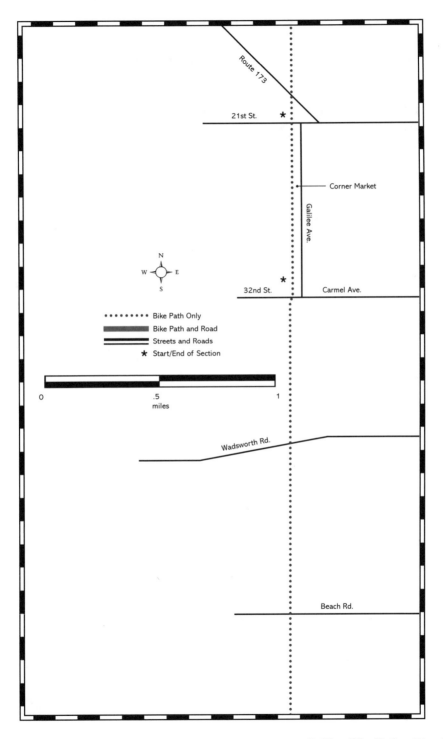

**SIDE TRIPS:** To Illinois Beach State Park North Unit (start is in following chapter) then south in park past the Power House to the South Unit of the Park and west again on Carmel Avenue to the intersection of the Zion and North Shore Bike Paths. 6.3 mile loop.

## DIRECTIONS (Mile marker/Description):

**0.0** Carmel Avenue and bike/walking path on the west side of Galilee Avenue. Paved. Continue north.

**0.9** Corner market for food and drinks on Galilee Avenue.

**1.5** 21st Street & Galilee Avenue. Zion paved bike/walking path ends, and the Lake County gravel bike path starts again.

# 9. Lake County Bike Path North

## *2.5 miles*

*This section of the continuous off-road bike path starts in Zion and ends at the state line. There are mileage markers every .5 mile.*

**ROUTE:** The bike path continues at 21st Street and Galilee Avenue in Zion. The path is a continuation of the Zion Bike Path along the same old railroad bed. At the state line, the path continues and goes over a bridge at Russell Road.

**SURFACE:** This is a crushed gravel path.

**TRAFFIC:** The bike traffic is very light at all times.

**POINTS OF INTEREST:** The Illinois/Wisconsin state line.

**FACILITIES:** None, not even off the trail.

**SIDE LIGHTS:** The rails-to-trails proceeds along the same line as the section to the south.

**ALTERNATIVES:** There are road options to the east or west of the trail but not worth the effort.

**OTHER INFORMATION:** A section of *Hiking and Biking in Lake County, Illinois* by Jim Hochgesang describes this route and other interconnected routes in Lake County.

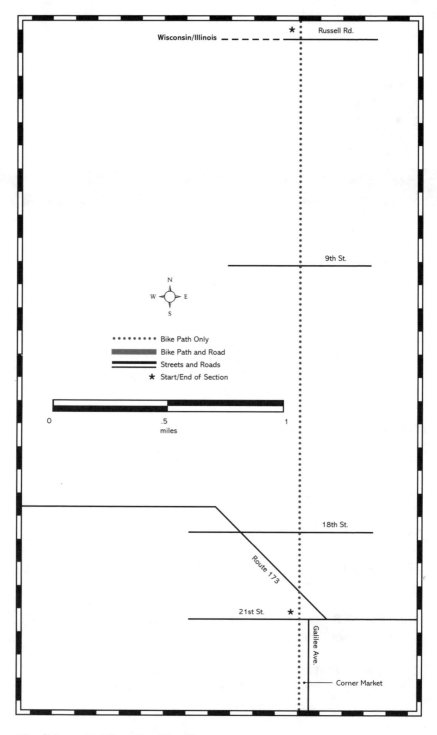

**PARKING:** There is plenty of parking but on the streets.

**SIDE TRIPS:** Near 17th Street, at the top of a hill, follow the bike path sign right (east) on Ravine Drive. The route is on the street until 18th Street and Gideon Streets, where a trail (paved) to Illinois State Park starts.

**DIRECTIONS (Mile marker/**Description)**:**

**0.0** 21st Street and Galilee Avenue on Lake County bike path. North on gravel path.

**0.1** Bridge over route 173.

**0.3** 18th Street.

**1.5** 9th Street.

**2.5** Over bridge at Russell Road; Wisconsin state line. You are now on the Kenosha County Bike Path. Surface the same.

## 10. Kenosha County Bike Path South

### *3.5 miles*

*This path, starting at the Illinois/Wisconsin state line, goes
3.5 miles to the south side of Kenosha and is the end of the
23.5-mile continuous series of bike paths that started at Fort
Sheridan in Highwood.*

**ROUTE:** From the state line to 30th Avenue and 89th Street on the
southwest side of the City of Kenosha. Straight north.

**SURFACE:** The Kenosha County Bike Path is crushed gravel. The path is a
little soft in areas.

**TRAFFIC:** Light bike use with few cross roads.

**POINTS OF INTEREST:** The Illinois/Wisconsin state line at Russell Road.

**FACILITIES:** None.

**SIDE LIGHTS:** It is very easy to miss the transition to the bike path in
Wisconsin.

**ALTERNATIVES:** It is possible to ride north along Lake Michigan by taking 116th Street (east) to 1st Avenue and then staying along the
lake to downtown Kenosha.

**OTHER INFORMATION:** A "Racine and Kenosha County Trails" map is

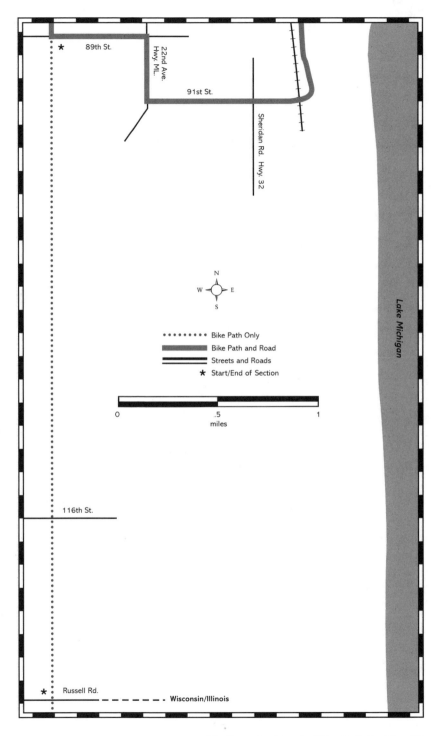

89th St.

22nd Ave.
Hwy. ML.

91st St.

Sheridan Rd. Hwy. 32

Lake Michigan

N
W ⊕ E
S

•••••••• Bike Path Only
Bike Path and Road
Streets and Roads
★ Start/End of Section

0          .5          1
miles

116th St.

Russell Rd.
– – – – – – – Wisconsin/Illinois

**10. Kenosha County Bike Path South**   51

available from some bike stores or:

American Bike Trails
1430 Main Street
Suite 525
Des Plaines, Illinois 60016

**PARKING:** There is no parking at the state line. The path goes over Russell Road on a bridge. There is safe street parking at the end of this bike trail, even for multiple days.

**SIDE TRIPS:** None.

**DIRECTIONS (Mile marker/**Description):

**0.0** Wisconsin/Illinois State Line at bridge over Russell Road. Continue north.

**1.0** Pass 116th Street (unmarked).

**3.5** 30th Avenue and 89th Street; south side of Kenosha. The bike path ends.

# 11. Kenosha

## *4.5 miles or 8.4 miles*

*Once again, you are between trails. However, the scenic route through Kenosha is a very enjoyable ride and recommended.*

**OPTION A:** Direct Route. Fastest route of limited interest. This route is virtually straight north along a wide road. 4.5 miles.

**OPTION B:** Scenic Route. Much slower but very interesting along the lakefront and through downtown. 8.4 miles.

**ROUTE:** The direct route is straight along 30th Avenue. This is absolutely the shortest route. The scenic route takes you east to Lake Michigan, north along the lake and then back west again to the trail. This route is pretty well marked and incorporates some bike trails through lakeside parks.

**SURFACE:** All on city streets except for the paved bike paths along the lake through the parks.

**TRAFFIC:** All the roads on both routes are quiet to moderately busy, depending on the time of day. Obviously, in the downtown area on the scenic route, there is heavier traffic on 6th Avenue.

**POINTS OF INTEREST:** On the direct route you pass the Chrysler Engine Plant, which at one time employed 5,000 but now employs 1,000. On the scenic route, you see the new boat marina, downtown Kenosha and excellent views of Lake Michigan.

**FACILITIES:** Plenty of restaurants and stores along both routes.

**SIDE LIGHTS:** The huge open space east of downtown is where the old Chrysler Plant once stood. This was the heart of the Kenosha economy, but the community has found a way to prosper without it. Also, at 1.2 miles you pass the Keno Drive-In Theatre. One of the very last of a disappearing venue. Also on the scenic route, at 4.5 miles, you pass Kemper Hall, which is a former women's prep school.

**ALTERNATIVES:** There are many options, but these are the two best. Some city streets north will eventually get you to the north bike path.

**OTHER INFORMATION:** The "Racine and Kenosha County Trails" map has a very generalized guide through the scenic route but is really of little value.

**PARKING:** At either end of this route section, street parking is available. It is safe and multiday use should be fine.

**SIDE TRIPS:** Out around the boat marina east of downtown.

**DIRECTIONS (Mile marker/**Description):

**0.0** 30th Avenue and 89th Street at end of bike path on south side of Kenosha. (See options.)

**OPTION A:** Direct Route. Fastest route of limited interest. This route is virtually straight north along a wide street 4.5 miles.

**OPTION B:** Scenic Route. Much slower but very interesting. Along the lakefront and through downtown 8.4 miles.

**DIRECT ROUTE (A)**

**0.0** Bike path ends at 30th Avenue and 89th Street, south side of Kenosha. Go north on 30th Avenue.

**1.0** Snap-On Drive.

**1.5** 76th Street. Total Cyclery just to the east on 76th Street.

**2.6** Pass the Chrysler Engine Plant, employed 5,000 before, now 1,000.

**4.4** 35th Street, right (east) for 2 blocks.

**4.5** Left (north), bike path toward Racine.

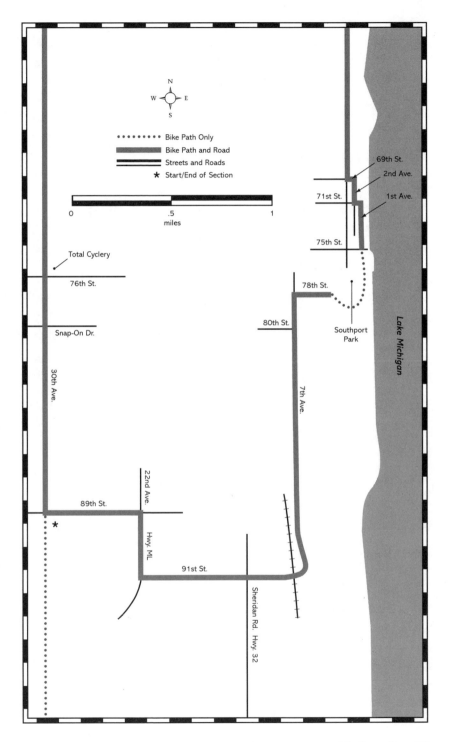

Bike Path Only
Bike Path and Road
Streets and Roads
★ Start/End of Section

0          .5          1
miles

69th St.
2nd Ave.
71st St.
1st Ave.
75th St.

Total Cyclery
76th St.
Snap-On Dr.

30th Ave.

78th St.
80th St.
Southport Park

Lake Michigan

7th Ave.

22nd Ave.
89th St.
Hwy. ML
91st St.

Sheridan Rd. Hwy. 32

## SCENIC ROUTE (B)

**0.0** 30th Avenue and 89th Street east along 89th Street and Anderson Park on bike path on north side of the street. (There is no bike route sign directing you to the lakefront.)

**0.5** Highway ML, right (south). Bike lane on shoulder.

**0.7** 91st Street, left (east).

**1.2** Sheridan Road (Highway 32).

**1.5** Cross railroad tracks.

**1.6** Road curves left (north) and becomes 7th Avenue. There are now bike route signs to downtown. The route is well marked. There is a bike lane.

**2.8** 80th and 7th Avenue continue north.

**3.1** 78th Street, right (east) and go to Lake Michigan. Follow the well-marked bike route signs, since the route is complex.

**3.3** 3rd Avenue, right (south) on road that curves east.

**3.4** Bike path, left (north) into park.

**3.7** 75th Street and 1st Avenue. Straight onto 1st Avenue.

**4.0** 71st Street, left (1st Avenue ends) to...

**4.0** 2nd Avenue, right (north) to...

**4.1** 69th Street, left (west) to...

**4.1** 3rd Avenue, right (north).

**4.5** Kemper Hall, former women's prep school.

**4.7** Path to lakefront through Eichelman Park. Right (east).

**4.9** Back to 3rd Avenue north to...

**5.2** 57th Street, left (west) to...

**5.3** 5th Avenue, right (north) to...

**5.4** 55th Street, left (west) to...

**5.5** 6th Avenue, right (north).

**5.6** Follow bike route over bridge. Angle into 7th Avenue.

**5.8** Ski and Sports Chalet bike shop.

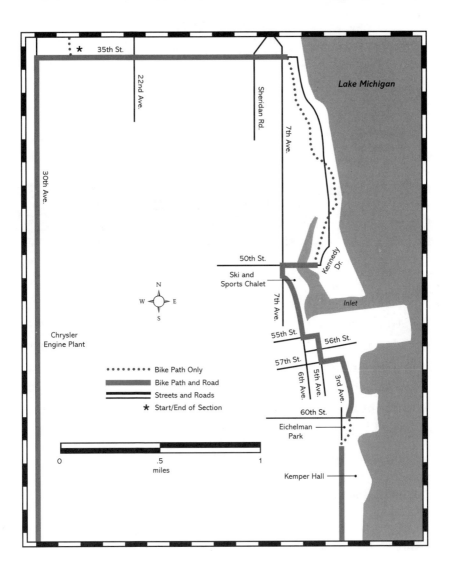

**5.9** 7th Avenue and 50th Street to right (east).

**6.0** Over bridge to Kennedy Drive, left (north) and immediately bear right (north) onto the bike path through the park.

**7.3** End of bike path at Kennedy Drive or 35th Street and 7th Avenue. Take 35th Street west (bike route).

**7.4** Sheridan Road.

**8.4** Bike trail right (north) to Racine. Gravel.

# 12. Kenosha County/ Racine County Bike Path

## 7.1 miles

*This bike path runs between north Kenosha and south Racine. This path does not run through either the City of Kenosha or the City of Racine. The scenery along this section is superior to that of the northern section of the Racine County Bike Path.*

**ROUTE:** The bike trail starts at 35th Street between 30th Avenue and 22nd Avenue in Kenosha and ends at West Avenue and 21st Street in Racine. This trail is a rails-to-trails conversion, so it is absolutely straight north/south.

**SURFACE:** The trail is crushed gravel that is well maintained. There are a few soft spots.

**TRAFFIC:** Bike traffic is very light. The cross roads are generally quiet and easy to cross.

**POINTS OF INTEREST:** Nice scenery.

**FACILITIES:** No water or bathrooms on the trail. At 1.3 miles, there is the Glenwood Crossings Shopping Center 3 blocks west of the trail.

**SIDE LIGHTS:** The Kenosha Country Club.

**ALTERNATIVES:** Highway 32 runs along Lake Michigan east of the bike

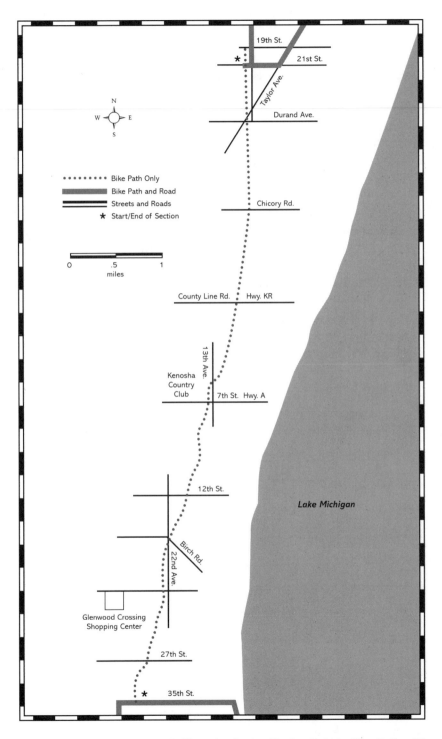

19th St.

21st St.

★

Taylor Ave.

Durand Ave.

N
W ● E
S

•••••••••• Bike Path Only
▨▨▨▨▨ Bike Path and Road
━━━━━ Streets and Roads
★ Start/End of Section

Chicory Rd.

0        .5        1
miles

County Line Rd.        Hwy. KR

13th Ave.

Kenosha
Country
Club            7th St. Hwy. A

12th St.

Lake Michigan

Birch Rd.

22nd Ave.

Glenwood Crossing
Shopping Center

27th St.

★ 35th St.

**12. Kenosha County/Racine County Bike Path  59**

path. There is traffic. You have to pick up the highway in the City of Kenosha and end in the City of Racine.

**OTHER INFORMATION:** A "Racine and Kenosha County Trails" map is available from some bike stores or:

American Bike Trails
1430 Main Street
Suite 525
Des Plaines, Illinois 60016

**PARKING:** At the south end of this trail, there is street parking in suburban areas. This parking is safe even for multiple days. Multiday parking at the north trailhead is not recommended.

**SIDE TRIPS:** The "Racine County Bicycle and Pedestrian Trails" map and the "Racine and Kenosha County Trails" map show road routes to the west toward Burlington.

**DIRECTIONS (Mile marker/**Description):
**0.0** 35th Street and start of bike trail on north side of Kenosha. North on gravel bike path.

**1.3** Pass Glenwood Shopping Center just west on cross roads off path. Restaurants, groceries, etc.

**1.9** Cross Birch Road and 22nd Street on path.

**2.4** 12th Street.

**3.5** Cross road.

**3.8** Kenosha Golf Course.

**4.6** Cross road.

**5.5** Cross Road (Chickory Road).

**6.6** Durand Avenue. Bike path narrows slightly.

**7.1** 21st Street in South Racine.

# 13. Racine

## *4.2 miles or 6.3 miles*

*The Racine County Bike Path does not pass through the City of Racine. The two options are either direct or through downtown Racine.*

**OPTION A:** Direct Route. 4.2 miles to bike path on north side of Racine. Fast, little of interest, somewhat unsafe. Be aware that you are near a high crime area.

**OPTION B:** Downtown Route. 6.3 miles to bike path on north side of Racine. Somewhat scenic and of more interest. Also safer.

**ROUTE:** Both routes are all on city streets. The downtown route takes you east to Lake Michigan through downtown Racine and finally west again to the bike path. The direct route is 2.1 miles shorter and faster along wide streets on the west side of the downtown area.

**SURFACE:** The whole route is on paved city streets.

**TRAFFIC:** The downtown route at certain hours can be busy on the main streets. Along Michigan Boulevard it is always quiet. The direct route is on main streets that carry traffic, but they are all four lanes. The quieter route is through downtown.

**POINTS OF INTEREST:** The downtown route is along the lake and near the new downtown boat marina. Downtown Racine has a lot of interesting historical buildings. At 1.7 miles, you pass Johnson Wax. The Landmark Tower office building was designed by Frank Lloyd Wright. The direct route has little of interest.

**FACILITIES:** Lots of restaurants, convenience stores on both routes.

**SIDE LIGHTS:** On the downtown route at Monument Square (1 block off the route to the west at 3.3 mile point) is the Recycles Bike Shop. This bike shop has a big inventory of used bikes with a total value of less than what your bike is probably worth.

**ALTERNATIVES:** You could take Highway 32 through downtown to Layard Avenue. Lots of traffic. If you chose the alternate route to Wind Point, you must take Highway 32 since there are no through routes on the north side of Racine.

**OTHER INFORMATION:** Neither the Racine County Bicycle and Pedestrian Trails Map nor the Racine and Kenosha County Trails Map help the cyclist through the city. City maps can be obtained from the Racine County Convention and Visitors Bureau at (800)CRACINE.

**PARKING:** There is parking on the lakefront in Racine for multiday use for the downtown route. For the direct route, you must take care for secure parking. Not recommended.

**SIDE TRIPS:** There are roads east of Main Street, downtown that go out to the boat marina on Lake Michigan.

**DIRECTIONS (Mile marker/**Description):
**DIRECT ROUTE (A)**
**0.0** 21st Street. Continue on bike path.

**0.3** Bike path ends at 19th Street. Take West Boulevard, the major road running parallel to the bike path on the right. Straight (north).

**1.3** Kinzie Avenue, right (east). Road curves North then east again.

**2.0** Road becomes 6th Street (east). Traffic.

**2.3** Memorial Drive, left (north). Busy road. Urban riding.

**2.7** State Street, straight on Memorial Drive. Economically depressed urban area.

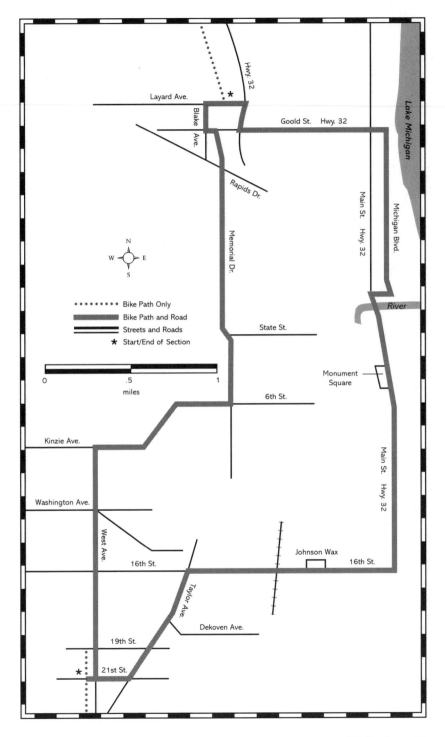

Hwy. 32

Layard Ave.

★

Blake Ave.

Goold St.    Hwy. 32

Rapids Dr.

Lake Michigan

Main St.    Hwy. 32

Michigan Blvd.

Memorial Dr.

N
W ⎯✧⎯ E
S

River

Bike Path Only
Bike Path and Road
Streets and Roads
★ Start/End of Section

State St.

0        .5            1
miles

Monument
Square

6th St.

Kinzie Ave.

Washington Ave.

West Ave.

16th St.

Main St.    Hwy. 32

Johnson Wax

16th St.

Taylor Ave.

Dekoven Ave.

19th St.

★

21st St.

**3.9** Goold Street, left (west) for 1 block to…

**4.0** Blake Street, right (north).

**4.1** Layand Avenue, right (east) for 1 block to start of bike path north.

**4.2** Bike path left (north).

## DOWNTOWN ROUTE (B)

**0.0** 21st Street, right (east) 2 blocks before the bike path ends.

**0.2** Taylor Avenue, left (northeast). Diagonal street. Major road. Traffic.

**0.6** DeKoven Avenue.

**1.0** 16th Street, right (east). Urban biking, share road.

**1.4** Railroad tracks.

**1.7** S.C. Johnson Company. Landmark Tower Office Building by Frank Lloyd Wright.

**2.3** Main Street, left (north). 16th Street ends at Lake bluff. Main Street is one way going north.

**2.5** 14th Street; end one way.

**2.7** 12th Street, right (east). 1 block then left (north) on Lake Avenue.

**2.9** 11th Street, cross onto cement walkway through park. Lochnaiar Inn on the corner of Lake Avenue and 11th Street.

**3.0** 10th Street, continue north on Lake Avenue.

**3.8** Gas Light Drive, left (west) 1 block.

**3.8** Main Street, right (north). This is downtown Racine.

**4.1** Dodge Street, right (east) just past bridge over Root River.

**4.2** Michigan Boulevard, left (north).

**5.2** Goold Street, left (west). Cross Main Street. Goold is Highway 32 after Main Street. Traffic.

**6.1** Douglas Avenue (Highway 32) right (north) for 1 block.

**6.2** Layard Avenue (sign hard to see), left (west) for 1 block.

**6.3** Bike path right (north) Racine County Bicycle Trail.

# 14. North Racine Bike Path

## 5.8 miles

*This bike path is on an old rail bed. The scenery is dull, along high electrical wire towers. It is straight and fast.*

**ROUTE:** This section is all on an off-street trail. You occasionally cross roads that are named after the distance from central Racine. The bike trail is straight and simple to follow. North of 7 Mile Road, the trail is not passable.

**SURFACE:** The trail has a crushed stone surface, which is generally firm and smooth. There is no problem for any kind of bike.

**TRAFFIC:** Very light bike traffic. The cross roads carry moderate traffic.

**POINTS OF INTEREST:** There are no points of interest on the bike trail itself. Side trips will take you to the pretty area of Wind Point or to Cliffside Park.

**FACILITIES:** There are no facilities along this 5.8-mile stretch of bike path. There is a convenience store two blocks east of the bike path on 4 Mile Road.

**SIDE LIGHTS:** None.

**ALTERNATIVES:** You can follow Highway 32 (Chicago Road/Douglas Road) out of Racine. This is a fast, direct route with traffic. Out of

Racine, a longer, more scenic route through Wind Point is available. Start on Main Street (north) to Michigan Boulevard to Light House Drive to Wind Point to 4 Mile Road to Charles Road to 5 ½ Mile Road to Novak Road to 6 Mile Road to Michina to 7 Mile Road to bike path.

**OTHER INFORMATION:** You can get two different maps of this bike path. Frankly, neither is of any real help. A "Racine County Bicycle and Pedestrian Trails" map is available from:

Racine County Public Works
14200 Washington Avenue
Sturtevant, Wisconsin 53177
(414) 886-8440

Also, a "Racine and Kenosha County Trails" map is available from some bike stores or:

American Bike Trails
1430 Main Street
Suite 525
Des Plaines, Illinois 60616

**PARKING:** There are no parking lots at either end of this trail section, although you can park on the street, but it is not recommended for multiday use.

**SIDE TRIPS:** The alternate route through Wind Point could also be considered a side trip. At 6 Mile Road, Cliffside County Park is to the east. Follow the signs directing you to the park.

**DIRECTIONS (Mile marker/**Description):

**0.0** Layard Avenue and start of bike path 1 ½ blocks west of Douglas Avenue in Racine. North.

**1.4** Cross road.

**2.6** 4 Mile Road, convenience store (Super America) to east off trail 2 blocks, snacks, drinks and restrooms.

**3.2** 4 ½ Mile Road and Douglas Avenue. Take sidewalk to 4 ½ Mile Road (150 feet), cross Douglas (Highway 32) and 4 ½ Mile Road. The

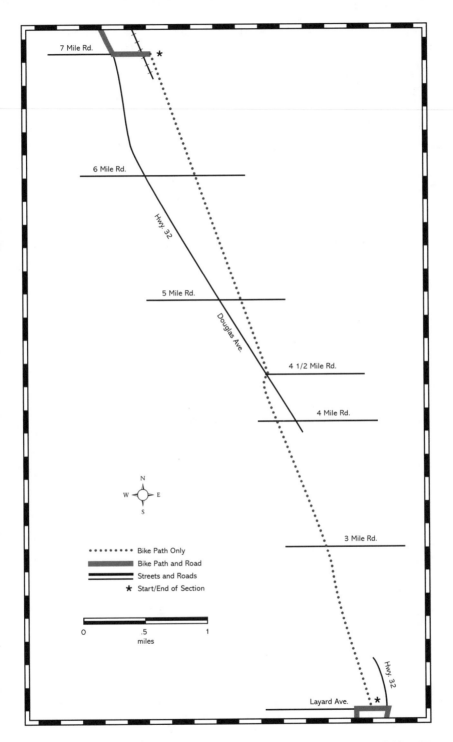

7 Mile Rd.

*

6 Mile Rd.

Hwy. 32

5 Mile Rd.

Douglas Ave.

4 1/2 Mile Rd.

4 Mile Rd.

N
W ⊕ E
S

•••••••• Bike Path Only

Bike Path and Road

Streets and Roads

★ Start/End of Section

0          .5          1
       miles

3 Mile Rd.

Hwy. 32

Layard Ave.          *

**14. North Racine Bike Path   67**

bike path continues on the right (east) side of Douglas Avenue (Highway 32).

**3.7** 5 Mile Road.

**4.8** 6 Mile Road. Possible side trip to Cliffside County Park.

**5.8** End of bike path at 7 Mile Road. Turn left (west).

# 15. North Racine To Oak Creek

## *6.9 miles*

*This section is the best available connector route between the Racine County Bike Route in Racine County and the Oak Leaf Bike Route in Milwaukee. The 3.3 miles on Highway 32 are travelled strictly to get you from Point A to Point B.*

**ROUTE:** 7 Mile Road is a country road. Highway 32 has a narrow shoulder. On Highway 32, there is no possible route to the east until you get to Ryan Road. From the intersection of Ryan Road and Chicago Road (Highway 32) until you reach Oak Creek Parkway you are on quiet roads through suburbs and industrial areas.

**SURFACE:** Paved streets. There are no bike paths of any sort in this section.

**TRAFFIC:** This is the toughest section of the whole trip. The 3.3 miles along Highway 32 are busy highway riding. There is a shoulder, but it is only 2 feet wide. Otherwise, the other roads are quiet to moderate in traffic.

**POINTS OF INTEREST:** Little of interest.

**FACILITIES:** There are tavern/restaurants along 5th Avenue in Oak Creek, and there are tavern/restaurants along Highway 32.

**SIDE TRIPS:** At Oak Creek Parkway, at the end of this route section, you

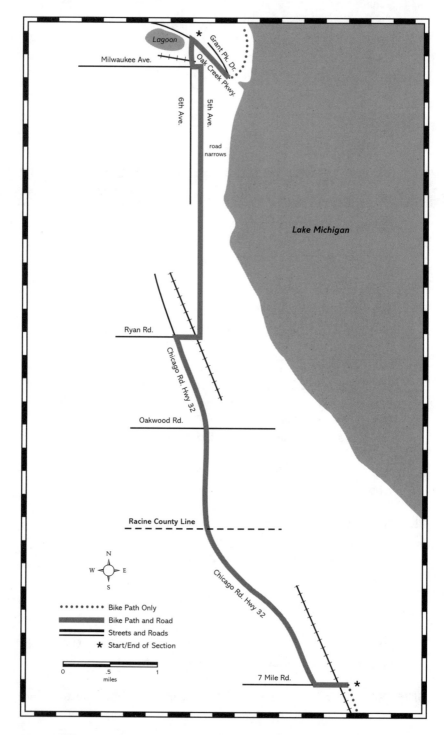

Lagoon

Grant Pk. Dr.

Oak Creek Pkwy.

Milwaukee Ave.

6th Ave.

5th Ave.

road narrows

Lake Michigan

Ryan Rd.

Chicago Rd. Hwy 32

Oakwood Rd.

Racine County Line

N
W E
S

Chicago Rd. Hwy 32

•••••••• Bike Path Only
Bike Path and Road
Streets and Roads
★ Start/End of Section

0    .5    1
miles

7 Mile Rd.

★

can take the Oak Leaf Bike Path, which circles back to downtown Milwaukee in 76 miles.

**ALTERNATIVES:** For a faster option, stay on Highway 32. This is fast riding, few stops and traffic.

**OTHER INFORMATION:** The only other information you might want in this section is a good map. The best map that shows all the minor roads that you travel is the Road Map of Southeastern Wisconsin available from:

Milwaukee Map Service Inc.
959 North Mayfair Road
Milwaukee, Wisconsin 53226
(800) 525-3822 or (414) 774-1300

**PARKING:** No long-term parking is available at either end of the route section. There is parking on 5th Avenue in Oak Creek and in parking lots for restaurants on Highway 32. Good parking in parking lots at the corner of Ryan Road and Chicago Road (Highway 32).

**SIDE TRIPS:** None of any interest.

**DIRECTIONS (Mile marker/**Description):

**0.0** 7 Mile Road at end of bike trail. 7 Mile Road west.

**0.4** Chicago Road (Highway 32), right (north); traffic, narrow shoulder.

**1.6** Milwaukee County/Racine County Line. Continue on Highway 32 North.

**2.7** Oakwood Road.

**3.7** Ryan Road, right (east). You are at Chicago Road 3800 E and Ryan Road 9500 S on the Milwaukee Grid.

**4.0** 5th Avenue, left (north) just after the railroad tracks. 5th Avenue is a narrow 2-lane road but generally has low traffic.

**5.5** 5th Avenue becomes wider through a residential area.

**6.8** 5th Avenue ends at Milwaukee Avenue, go left (west) 1 block to 6th Avenue and turn right (north). Go down the hill under the railroad bridge and over the bridge over the creek.

**6.9** Oak Creek Parkway, turn right.

# 16. Oak Leaf Bike Path

## *8.8 miles*

*95% of this route is off-road, paved bike path. The route is a section of the Oak Leaf Bike Route, which circles Milwaukee. This route was previously called the '76 Route. In places the signs are hard to spot. This is a great ride with views of Lake Michigan, downtown Milwaukee and multiple lakefront parks.*

**ROUTE:** This route section starts at Oak Creek Parkway and 6th Avenue just east of the lagoon. Take the Oak Leaf ('76) Trail north. If you lose the path, just stay next to the lake bluff and you will pick up the signs for the Bike Trail. The path and route always runs east of Lake Drive (Highway 32) through South Milwaukee, Cudahy, St. Francis and Milwaukee. There are signs that direct you, but occasionally they are missing. This section ends at the South Shore Yacht Club parking lot. South Shore Yacht Club is approximately 5 miles southeast of downtown.

**SURFACE:** The bike path is fully paved and generally in good condition. If you choose the beach route option at 7.5 miles, the surface is gravel and some rough paved sections.

**TRAFFIC:** Generally, the bike path is relatively quiet for a suburban path. The road part of the route is on quiet roads.

**POINTS OF INTEREST:** Grant Park Club House is a quaint house with nice gardens and places to rest. Harnischfeger's new and dramatic office setting is on Lake Michigan's bluff. There are excellent views of downtown Milwaukee. The whole south shore area is park land. At times you will feel that you are in the country.

**FACILITIES:** Grant Park's Club House has a club house for snacks, drinks and restrooms. Warnimont Golf Course has the same. There are water and restrooms in the park just before South Shore Yacht Club. The White House, 2900 S. Kinnickinnic Avenue, just west of South Shore Yacht Club is the best place in town for postride refreshments.

**SIDE LIGHTS:** If you choose the beach route option, the '76 route went this way until the high-water cycle of Lake Michigan in the late '80s washed out the old path. The water has receded, but the path now is gravel and the main route continues up onto the bluff. Milwaukee has a huge portion of its space devoted to parks, and you have passed through some of its finest on this route.

**ALTERNATIVES:** There is an alternate, faster route to the South Shore Yacht Club that is 2.2 miles shorter. Generally straight, fast, wide with moderate traffic. At the start of this route section, continue north on 6th Avenue past Oak Creek Parkway and then jog right (east) for 150 feet to Lake Drive. Take Lake Drive north.

**OTHER INFORMATION:** There are occasional posted maps showing the bike route and your location. Also, at times, bike route maps are available at the park offices along the way. The maps are available from the Milwaukee County Park System, (414) 257-6100. These maps show the whole Oak Leaf Path, which previously was called '76 bike trail.

**PARKING:** There is plenty of parking in any of the parks along the route. There is plenty of public parking in the lot at the South Shore Yacht Club and the adjacent beach. Multiday parking is safe.

**SIDE TRIPS:** a) Because you are on the Oak Leaf Bike Path, which forms a loop within Milwaukee County, you can extend your bike trip from either end of this section and continue on the bike trail.

b) South Shore Yacht Club to Greenfield Park on Milwaukee's West Side. This route connects in turn with the Waukesha Bike Trail, which

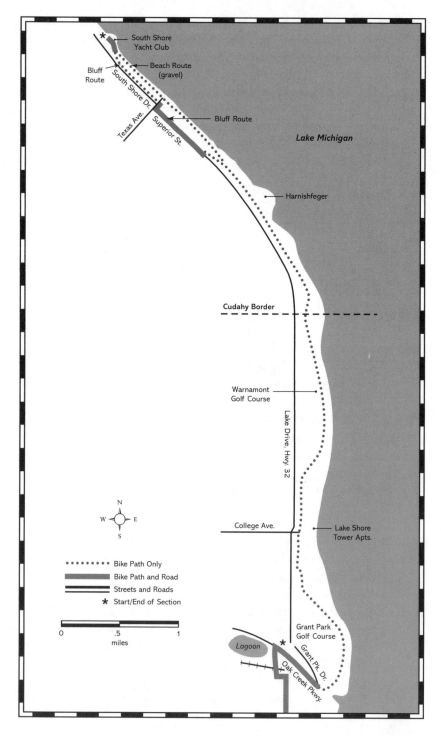

South Shore
Yacht Club

Beach Route
(gravel)

Bluff
Route

South Shore Dr.

Texas Ave.

Superior St.

Bluff Route

Lake Michigan

Harnishfeger

Cudahy Border

Warnamont
Golf Course

Lake Drive, Hwy. 32

College Ave.

Lake Shore
Tower Apts.

N
W ⊕ E
S

• • • • • • • • •  Bike Path Only

Bike Path and Road

Streets and Roads

★  Start/End of Section

0        .5        1
miles

Grant Park
Golf Course

Lagoon

Grant Pk. Dr.

Oak Creek Pkwy.

74   **Chicago to Milwaukee (North)**

takes you to Madison along a gravel off-road trail. See side route descriptions.

**DIRECTIONS (Mile marker/**Description):

**0.0**  Oak Creek Parkway and 6th Avenue just east of lagoon. You are now on the Oak Leaf Bike Trail, which was formerly known as the '76 Trail. Go east.

**0.8**  Grant Park Golf Course Club House. From the golf course the bike trail heads north along the lake bluff.

**2.9**  Lake Shore Tower Apartments, College Avenue, leave South Milwaukee and enter Cudahy.

**4.4**  Pass Warnimont Golf Course.

**6.3**  Pass future planned community on the lake shore; future hotel, apartments, condos, houses and retail.

**7.2**  Pass Harnischfeger Industries, new dramatic offices.

**7.5**  Y in path. 2 options.

**BLUFF ROUTE (A):** Stay left (straight) at Y in path. Follow signs for the Bike Path along Bluff. Path swings out along Shore Drive. Use sidewalk to Texas Street. Go right (east) to Lake Drive; left (north) follow path down to the lake level.

**BEACH ROUTE (B):** Go right (slightly east) down the hill on the path to the beach. Rough (but usable) path along the shore. Go past water station to beach and rejoin upper bike trail. This was the former '76 Trail until lake levels washed it out in the late 1980's.

**8.5**  Paths merge.

**8.8**  South Shore Yacht Club, 2300 East Nock Street, Milwaukee.

# 17. Milwaukee

## 4.7 miles

*This is an urban/industrial bike ride on city streets. The area covered is the same distance covered by the Hoan Bridge, which is off limits to bicycles. This route avoids most of the downtown area by finishing on the east side of the downtown.*

**ROUTE:** This route section starts at the north end of the South Shore Yacht Club parking lot and goes .3 miles on the bike path north, then onto city streets. This is a somewhat circuitous route, avoiding the worst of the traffic. The route ends at the north end of Henry Maier Festival Park, which is on Lake Michigan east of downtown.

**SURFACE:** City streets, which are generally well maintained. You cross some railroad tracks and bridges that have gaps.

**TRAFFIC:** The worst of the traffic is avoided. Russell Avenue is a 2-lane road that handles a lot of traffic at times. First Street is a busy road during the week but it is 4 lanes.

**POINTS OF INTEREST:** The Allen Bradley Plant, on top of which is the second largest 4-sided clock in the world (after Big Ben in London). Henry Maier Festival Park, which is the site of Summerfest and many ethnic festivals. Milwaukee downtown.

**FACILITIES:** Basically no water or restrooms since you are traveling through industrial Milwaukee. Drinks and food at Groppi Grocery

Store on Russell Avenue. There are a number of bar/restaurants along the way. There is a convenience store on 1st Street.

**SIDE LIGHTS:** The Hoan Bridge, which is the direct route to downtown Milwaukee, is also known as "The Bridge to Nowhere". The Groppi Grocery Store is owned by the Groppi Family. Father James Groppi was a locally famous civil rights leader in Milwaukee in the '60s and '70s.

**ALTERNATIVES:** At 3.5 miles, you can continue north on 1st Street, which becomes Water Street and goes to the heart of downtown. This is a shorter route, but has more traffic.

**OTHER INFORMATION:** The map for the Oak Leaf Bike Path ('76 Route) is available from the Milwaukee County Park System (414) 257-6100.

**PARKING:** There is plenty of parking in the South Shore Yacht Club parking lot. South of downtown on the east side are a number of low-cost parking lots. These lots seem secure for multiday parking.

**SIDE TRIPS:** a) The lakefront north of downtown has some pretty bike paths through the parks.

b) The Oak Leaf Bike Path starts on the northeast side of downtown and eventually goes north along the Milwaukee River to the northern suburbs.

c) The lakefront paths run into Lake Drive (Highway 32), which is a 4-lane road north through the north shore suburbs. Timing is important in riding on Lake Drive since this is a commuter route.

d) A full day ride on the Oak Leaf Bike Path around the City of Milwaukee through dozens of parks. 76 miles.

**DIRECTIONS (Mile marker/Description):**

**0.0** South Shore Yacht Club (parking lot). Go north through the parking lot and follow bike trail sign.

**0.3** Bike trail swings left (west) and ends at Lincoln Memorial Drive and Russell Avenue. Straight (west) on Russell Avenue.

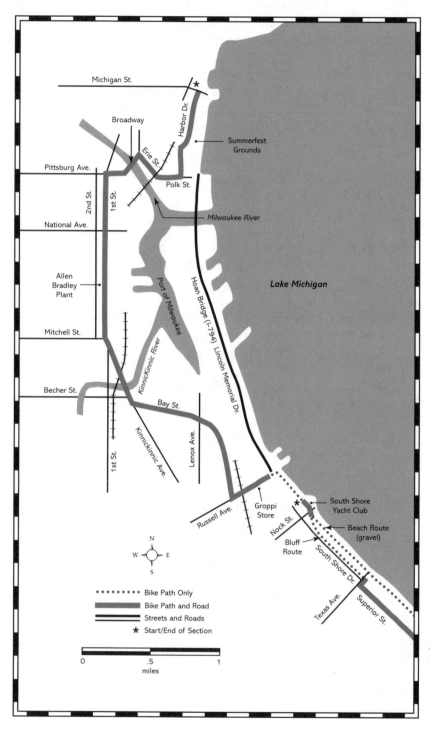

Michigan St.

Broadway

Pittsburg Ave.

Erie St.

Harbor Dr.

*

Summerfest
Grounds

Polk St.

2nd St.

1st St.

*Milwaukee River*

National Ave.

Allen
Bradley
Plant

Port of Milwaukee

Hoan Bridge (I-794)

Lincoln Memorial Dr.

*Lake Michigan*

Mitchell St.

KinnicKinnic River

Becher St.

Bay St.

Kinnickinnic Ave.

1st St.

Lenox Ave.

Russell Ave.

Groppi
Store

Nock St.

*

South Shore
Yacht Club

Beach Route
(gravel)

Bluff
Route

South Shore Dr.

Texas Ave.

Superior St.

N
W      E
S

•••••••• Bike Path Only

Bike Path and Road

Streets and Roads

★ Start/End of Section

0          .5          1
miles

**0.5** Groppi Grocery Store.

**0.7** Right (north) Bay Street after railroad tracks overhead.

**1.3** Cross Lenox Street.

**1.8** Right (north) on Kinnickinnic Avenue (KK Ave.). (This is industrial riding.)

**2.0** Over Kinnickinnic River.

**2.1** Under railroad trestle.

**2.3** Bear right (north) at Mitchell Street. KK Ave. runs into 1st Street, 4 lanes, urban traffic. Go on 1st Street (north).

**2.7** Allen Bradley Plant.

**3.1** National Avenue.

**3.5** Pittsburg Avenue, right (east). Jog left (north) and cross the Milwaukee River.

**3.8** Right (east) Erie Street.

**4.0** Left (east) Polk Street just after crossing railroad tracks.

**4.1** Left (north) Harbor Drive.

**4.5** Main entrance to Summerfest Grounds.

**4.7** Left (west) on Michigan Street. 100 feet west is Lincoln Memorial Drive. This is the east side of downtown Milwaukee.

# 18. Excursion

## 13.2 miles

*This is a surprisingly good ride through an urban/industrial
area. There are a few areas where the route is strictly useful to
connect the better sections. Through the middle part of the route
you pass through more parks and parkways along the
Kinnickinnic River. You follow a narrow green belt along the
river, which does snake around a little.*

**ROUTE:** This side trip actually branches off the Milwaukee section of the
route at the intersection of Russell Avenue and Bay Street. From
downtown you drive on Bay Street, which dead ends at Russell
Avenue. This route goes west on Russell Avenue while the route to
South Shore Yacht Club goes east on Russell Avenue. 95% of the
route is on city streets with a few bike paths through the parks. This
route is marked as the "76 EW" Trail. The EW is for east-west and
connects the Oak Leaf Path on the east side to the Oak Leaf Path
on the west side.

**SURFACE:** The bike paths through the parks are all paved. Otherwise,
you are on city streets.

**TRAFFIC:** Russell Avenue is a busy 2-lane road. The traffic can be heavy
on Howell Avenue and Chase Avenue, but these are short connector
routes. The parkways are quiet.

**POINT OF INTEREST:** Bay View, where urban life is still uncomplicated, civil and relatively crime free. Jackson Park is a beautiful central urban park with a pretty lagoon. Greenfield Park is a large west side park.

**FACILITIES:** Water and restrooms in Jackson Park and Greenfield Park. Some stores in Bay View (east part of route). At 108th Street (Highway 100) you will find all facilities on a busy street. Greenfield Park also has a snack bar at the golf course. At Cleveland and 92nd Street (10.1 mile mark), there is a deli store.

**SIDE LIGHTS:** Forest Home Cemetery is just north of the route between 20th Street and 27th (Layton Avenue). This is one of the oldest cemeteries in Milwaukee, and they have a hall of history within the grounds.

**ALTERNATIVES:** a) Lincoln Avenue is a straight shot to Greenfield Park. It is a colorful street that cuts across the south side. This is an urban route. Lincoln Avenue is about 5 blocks north of Russell Avenue.

b) When Kinnickinnic Parkway meanders between Jackson Park and McCarty Park (about 80th Street), Cleveland Avenue is a quiet and straight alternative if you want to save time.

**OTHER INFORMATION:** Most of this route is on the 76 EW route. The Oak Leaf Bike Path map is available from the Milwaukee County Park System, (414) 257-6100.

Also, a good map of Milwaukee is put out by:
Metropolitan Association of Commerce
765 North Milwaukee Street
Milwaukee, Wisconsin 53202
(414) 287-4100

**PARKING:** In the parking lot in front of the South Shore Yacht Club. Also in Greenfield Park there is a parking lot for the golf course. There is parking on the street along the whole route.

**SIDE TRIPS:** a) From Greenfield Park, through which the west leg of the Oak Leaf Bike Path passes, you can pedal north or south through a chain of parks. You could loop back to the east side by following the

Oak Leaf Bike Path since it circles back to the east on the north and south sides.

b) The New Berlin Recreational Trail. It takes you to the Waukesha County Bike Trail, through the City of Waukesha by roads to the trail that continues on to the east side of Madison.

## DIRECTIONS (Mile marker/Description):

**0.0** South Shore Yacht Club (parking lot). Go north through the parking lot and follow the bike trail sign.

**0.3** Bike trail swings left (west) and ends at Lincoln Memorial Drive and Russell Avenue. Straight (west) on Russell Avenue.

**0.5** Groppi Grocery Store.

**0.7** Cross Bay Street. (To go to downtown Milwaukee, see Route #1.)

**0.9** Kinnickinnic Avenue and Logan Avenue and Russell Avenue. Bear left (south) on Logan Avenue. Go one block south to

**0.9** Montana Street, right (west) immediately.

**1.4** Howell Avenue, right (north) for 150 feet.

**1.4** Montana Street, left (west).

**1.6** Austin Street, left (south) for 150 feet.

**1.6** Montana Street, right (west).

**1.8** Chase Avenue, right (north).

**2.0** Rosedale Avenue, left (west) before the railroad bridge.

**2.1** Under the freeway (Interstate 94).

**2.2** Bike trail. Bear right and follow the signs ('76 EW)

**2.3** 6th Street, left (south).

**2.6** Manitoba Street, right (west).

**3.5** 17th Street. Manitoba Street ends. Go straight (west) onto bike path, which is a continuation of the sidewalk on Manitoba Street.

**3.7** 20th Street, right (north). (The bike path ends.) 1 block.

**3.7** Kinnickinnic Parkway, left (west).

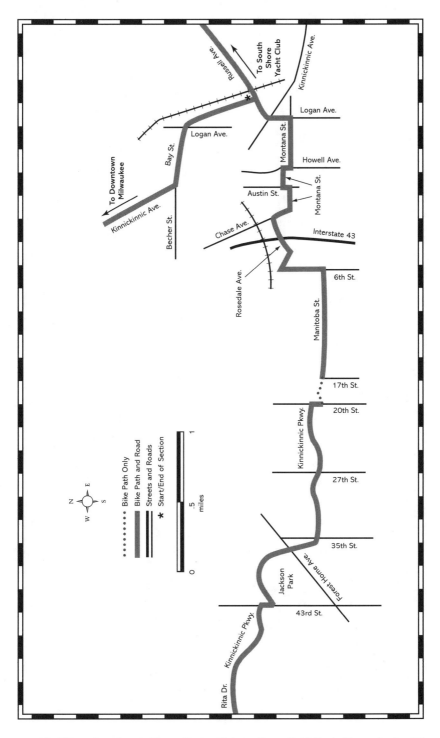

**18. Milwaukee South Shore Yacht Club to Greenfield Park (Excursion)** 83

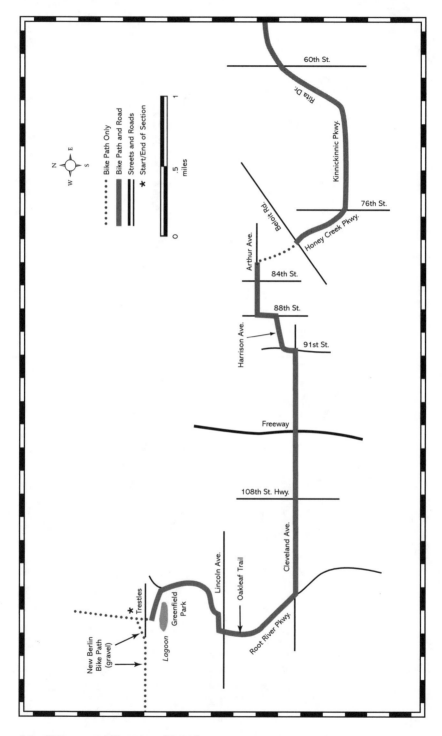

**4.3** Cross 27th Street.

**4.9** Cross 35th Street.

**5.1** Cross Forest Home Avenue, then into Jackson Park.

**5.7** 43rd Street, right (north) for 1 block.

**5.7** Kinnickinnic River Parkway, left (west) This curvy road becomes Rita Drive. Straight (west).

**7.0** Cross 60th Street. Rita Drive becomes Kinnickinnic Parkway again. Straight (west).

**8.4** Cross 76th Street. Now on Honey Creek Parkway. Straight (west).

**8.7** Cross Beloit Road. Bike path enters straight (west) into park. Path curves north.

**9.1** Arthur Avenue, left (west). (Bike path ends.)

**9.4** Cross 84th Street on Arthur Avenue. (Here you leave the 76 EW Bike Trail, which goes north on 84th Street and heads toward Wauwatosa.)

**9.6** 88th Street, left (south).

**9.8** Harrison Avenue, right (west).

**10.0** 91st Street, left (south). 1 block south.

**10.1** Cleveland Avenue, right (west).

**10.7** Over freeway.

**11.1** 108th Street (Highway 100). All services.

**11.9** Root River Parkway, right (north). This is now the Oak Leaf (76) Trail.

**12.0** Bear right (still north) at the stop sign on the unmarked road. (This is Root River Parkway.)

**12.6** Cross Lincoln Avenue on Root River Parkway and enter Greenfield Park. Road snakes through the park, initially heading east.

**12.9** Bear left (north) at the stop sign. Pass through forest.

**13.3** Left (west) on unmarked road passing the lagoon on the north side.

**13.7** Bike trail, right (north). Bike trail just before the stop sign under two very low railroad trestles.

**13.8** New Berlin Recreational Trail, left (west).

# Milwaukee to Chicago (South)

## Overview

**1. MILWAUKEE  4.7 miles**
Downtown Milwaukee to South Shore Yacht Club on the Oak Leaf (76) Bike Route.

**2. OAK LEAF BIKE PATH  8.8 miles**
South Shore Yacht Club to Grant Park (Oak Creek).

**3. OAK CREEK TO NORTH RACINE  6.9 miles**
Connector between Oak Leaf Bike Path and Racine County Bike Path.

**4. NORTH RACINE BIKE PATH  5.8 miles**
Crushed gravel county-maintained bike path.

**5. RACINE**
  a) Direct Route 4.2 miles.
  b) Downtown Route 6.3 miles.

**6. RACINE COUNTY/KENOSHA COUNTY BIKE PATH  7.1 miles**
The two county paths connect.

**7. KENOSHA**
  a) Direct Route 4.5 miles.
  b) Scenic Route 8.4 miles.

8. **KENOSHA COUNTY BIKE PATH SOUTH 3.5 miles**
Start of bike path to the Wisconsin/Illinois state line.

9. **LAKE COUNTY BIKE PATH NORTH 2.5 miles**
State line to the end of the county path.

10. **ZION BIKE PATH 1.5 miles**
Connects the north and south county bike paths.

11. **LAKE COUNTY BIKE PATH SOUTH 9.7 miles**
From Zion to Great Lakes Naval Station.

12. **NORTH SHORE BIKE PATH NORTH 6.3 miles**
Great Lakes Naval Station to end of path in Highwood.

13. **HIGHWOOD CONNECTOR ROUTE 1.5 miles**
North Shore Path does not run through Highwood.

14. **LAKE SHORE BIKE PATH SOUTH 11.1 miles**
Sporadic path and connector routes through the north suburbs.

15. **EVANSTON 5.3 miles**
Street route to Northwestern University bike paths to Chicago border.

16. **CHICAGO STREET CONNECTION 3.4 miles**
On city streets to connect with bike path to Loop.

17. **LAKE FRONT BIKE PATH 9.1 miles**
Ending at Loop along the lakefront on bike path.

18. **EXCURSION 8.5 miles**
a) Lake Shore Bike Path South in Chicago.

# 1. Milwaukee

## *4.7 miles*

*This is an urban/industrial bike ride on city streets. This route avoids most of the downtown area by starting on the east side of the downtown. The area covered is the same distance covered by the Hoan Bridge, which is off limits to bicycles.*

**ROUTE:** Start at the north end of Henry Maier Festival Park, which is on Lake Michigan east of downtown. This is a somewhat circuitous route avoiding the worst of the traffic. Only the last .3 miles is on a bike path.

**SURFACE:** City streets, which are generally well maintained. You cross some railroad tracks and bridges that have gaps.

**TRAFFIC:** The worst of the traffic is avoided. First Street is a busy road during the week but it is 4 lanes. Russell Avenue is a 2-lane road that handles a lot of traffic at times.

**POINTS OF INTEREST:** Milwaukee downtown. Henry Maier Festival Park, which is the site of Summerfest and many ethnic festivals. The Allen Bradley Plant, on top of which is the second largest 4-sided clock in the world (after Big Ben in London).

**FACILITIES:** Basically no water or restrooms since you are traveling through industrial Milwaukee. There is a convenience store on 1st Street. There are a number of bar/restaurants along the way. Drinks and food at Groppi Grocery Store on Russell Avenue.

**SIDE LIGHTS:** The Hoan Bridge, which is the direct route to South Shore Yacht Club, is also known as "The Bridge to Nowhere". The Groppi Grocery Store is owned by the Groppi Family. Father James Groppi was a locally famous civil rights leader in Milwaukee in the '60s and '70s.

**ALTERNATIVES:** From downtown you can go straight south on Water Street or other streets east of Water Street. Water Street becomes 1st Street. This is a shorter route, but has more traffic.

**OTHER INFORMATION:** The map for the Oak Leaf Bike Path ('76 Route) is available from the Milwaukee County Park System (414) 257-6100.

**PARKING:** South of downtown on the east side are a number of low-cost parking lots. These lots seem secure for multiday parking.

**SIDE TRIPS:** a) The lakefront north of downtown has some pretty bike paths through the parks.

b) The Oak Leaf Bike Path starts on the northeast side of downtown and eventually goes north along the Milwaukee River to the northern suburbs.

c) The lakefront paths run into Lake Drive (Highway 32), which is a 4-lane road north through the north shore suburbs. Timing is important in riding on Lake Drive since this is a commuter route.

d) A full day ride on the Oak Leaf Bike Path around the City of Milwaukee through dozens of parks. 76 miles.

**DIRECTIONS (Mile marker/**Description):
**0.0** Michigan Street and Lincoln Memorial Drive. East on Michigan Street 100 feet. Right (south) on Harbor Drive.

**0.3** Main entrance to Summerfest Grounds.

**0.6** Polk Street, right (west). (Harbor Drive ends.)

**0.7** Erie Street, right (north); immediately cross the railroad tracks.

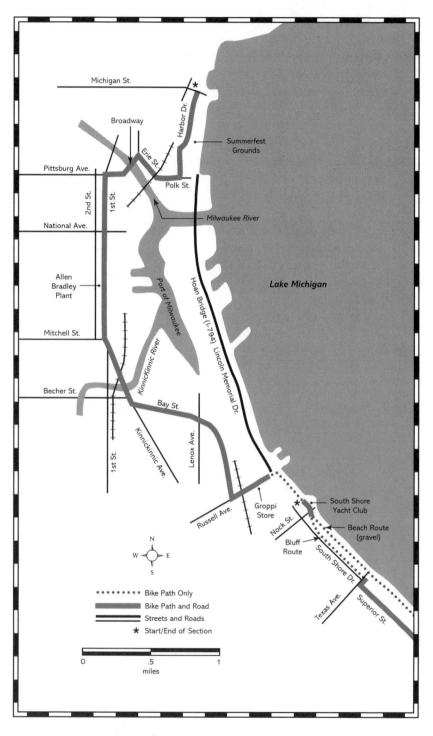

Michigan St.

Broadway

Harbor Dr.

Erie St.

Summerfest
Grounds

Pittsburg Ave.

2nd St.

1st St.

Polk St.

National Ave.

Milwaukee River

Allen
Bradley
Plant

Port of Milwaukee

Lake Michigan

Hoan Bridge (I-794) Lincoln Memorial Dr.

Mitchell St.

KinnicKinnic River

Becher St.

Bay St.

1st St.

Kinnickinnic Ave.

Lenox Ave.

Russell Ave.

Groppi
Store

Nock St.

South Shore
Yacht Club

Beach Route
(gravel)

Bluff
Route

South Shore Dr.

N
W ✶ E
S

Texas Ave.

Superior St.

•••••••• Bike Path Only

Bike Path and Road

Streets and Roads

✶ Start/End of Section

0       .5       1
miles

90   Milwaukee to Chicago (South)

**0.9** Broadway, left (west) at stop light. Over the bridge over the Milwaukee River. Street becomes Pittsburg Avenue and bears to the right.

**1.2** 1st Street, left (South). Four lanes, urban traffic. The Oak Leaf Bike Route is on 2nd Street (one block farther west), but 1st Street is just as good.

**1.6** Cross National Avenue.

**2.0** Allen Bradley Plant.

**2.4** Kinnickinnic Avenue, bear left (east) at Mitchell Street. 1st Street bears right.

**2.6** Under railroad trestle.

**2.7** Over Kinnickinnic River.

**2.9** Becher Street/Bay Street, left (east). (Becher Street becomes Bay Street east of Kinnickinnic Avenue.) This is industrial riding.

**3.4** Cross Lenox Street on Bay Street, which bears right (south).

**4.0** Russell Avenue, left (east) (Bay Street ends) immediately under the railroad tracks.

**4.2** Groppi Grocery Store.

**4.4** Lincoln Memorial Drive and Russell Avenue. Straight (east) toward the lake is the bike path. The path goes down and swings right (south along the lake).

**4.7** South Shore Yacht Club (parking lot).

# 2. Oak Leaf Bike Path

## *8.8 miles*

*95% of this route is off-road, paved bike path. The route is a section of the Oak Leaf Bike Route, which circles Milwaukee. This route was previously called the '76 Route. In places the signs are hard to spot. This is a great ride with views of Lake Michigan, downtown Milwaukee and multiple lakefront parks.*

**ROUTE:** This section starts at the South Shore Yacht Club parking lot. South Shore Yacht Club is approximately 5 miles southeast of downtown. Take the Oak Leaf ('76) Path south. If you lose the path, just stay next to the lake bluff and you will pick up the signs for the Oak Leaf Bike Path. The path and route always runs east of Lake Drive (Highway 32) through Milwaukee, St. Francis, Cudahy and South Milwaukee. There are signs that direct you but occasionally they are missing. After Grant Park, you take the park road west for the last $\frac{8}{10}$ of a mile.

**SURFACE:** The bike path is fully paved and generally in good condition. If you choose the beach option at 0.3 miles south of the parking lot, the surface is gravel and some rough paved sections.

**TRAFFIC:** Generally, the bike path is relatively quiet for a suburban path. The road part of the route is on quiet roads.

**POINTS OF INTEREST:** The whole south shore area is park land. At times you will feel that you are in the country. Facing north, there are excellent views of downtown Milwaukee. Harnischfeger's new and dramatic office setting on Lake Michigan's bluff. Grant Park Club House is a quaint house with nice gardens and places to rest.

**FACILITIES:** There are water and restrooms in the park just south of South Shore Yacht Club. Warnimont Golf Course has a club house for snacks, drinks and restrooms. Also, Grant Park's Club House has the same. The White House, 2900 S. Kinnickinnic Avenue, just west of South Shore Yacht Club, is the best place in town for postride refreshments.

**SIDE LIGHTS:** If you choose the beach route option, the '76 route went this way until the high-water cycle of Lake Michigan in the late '80s washed out the old path. The water has receded, but the path now is gravel and the main route goes up onto the bluff. Milwaukee has a huge portion of its space devoted to parks, and you will pass through some of its finest on this route.

**ALTERNATIVES:** There is an alternate faster route. From the South Shore Yacht Club, take Lake Drive. Generally straight, fast, wide with moderate traffic. It's 2.2 miles shorter to intersection of Chicago Road and Ryan Road. 9.8 miles versus 12.0 miles.

**OTHER INFORMATION:** There are occasional posted maps showing the bike route and your location. Also, at times, bike route maps are available at the park offices along the way. The maps are available from the Milwaukee County Park System, (414) 257-6100. These maps show the whole Oak Leaf Path, which previously was called '76 bike trail.

**PARKING:** There is plenty of public parking in the lot at the South Shore Yacht Club and the adjacent beach. Multiday parking is safe. Also, along the route there is plenty of parking in any of the parks.

**SIDE TRIPS:** a) Because you are on the Oak Leaf Bike Path, which forms a loop within Milwaukee County, you can extend your bike trip from either end of this section and continue on the bike trail.

b) South Shore Yacht Club to Greenfield Park on Milwaukee's West Side. This route connects in turn with the Waukesha Bike Trail, which

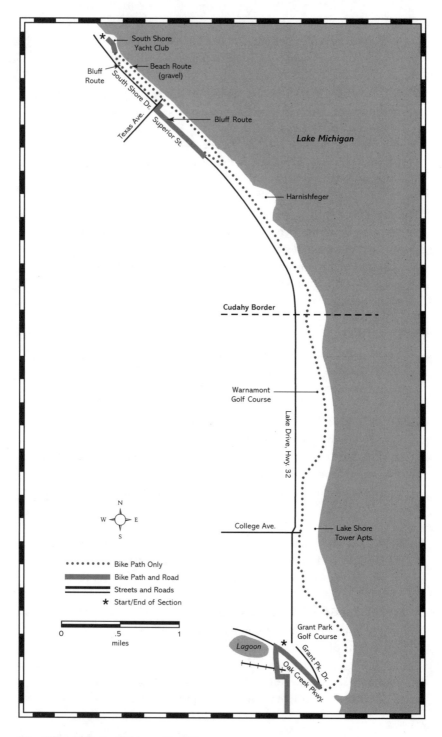

South Shore Yacht Club

Beach Route (gravel)

Bluff Route

South Shore Dr.

Bluff Route

Texas Ave.

Superior St.

Lake Michigan

Harnishfeger

Cudahy Border

Warnamont Golf Course

Lake Drive, Hwy. 32

N
W   E
S

College Ave.

Lake Shore Tower Apts.

Bike Path Only
Bike Path and Road
Streets and Roads
* Start/End of Section

0   .5   1
miles

Grant Park Golf Course

Lagoon

Grant Pk. Dr.

Oak Creek Pkwy.

takes you to Madison along a gravel off-road trail. See side route descriptions.

**DIRECTIONS (Mile marker/**Description):

**0.0** South Shore Yacht Club, 2300 East Nock Street, Milwaukee.

**0.0** Take bike/walkway at the south end of the parking lot (runs along the beach). Look back, excellent views of downtown Milwaukee.

**0.3** Two options:

> **BEACH ROUTE (A):** Take the path along the beach. Gravel surface along the beach, good views. Don't go up the bluff.

> **BLUFF ROUTE (B):** Follow signs up the bluff to South Shore Drive; go to the end. Go right (west) 1 block to Superior Street, then left along the sidewalk on east side of street (well marked).

**1.3** If on the beach route, eventually climb up the bluff to join the bike path. The distance is equal for either route.

**1.6** New dramatic office of Harnischfeger Industries.

**2.5** New planned hotel, apartments, condos, houses and retail on the lake. The trail is alongside of Lake Drive (Highway 32).

**2.8** Cudahy border line.

**4.4** Warnimont Golf Course.

**5.9** Lake Shore Tower Apartments, College Avenue; enter South Milwaukee.

**8.0** Grant Park Golf Course. Follow the Oak Leaf Route from Grant Park. The route follows the road that goes through the ravine heading west, Oak Creek Parkway (not the road just south of the golf course, Grant Park Drive.)

**8.8** There is a stop sign before the lagoon at the first cross road. No road sign. Go left (south). You now leave the Oak Leaf Bike Path, which continues straight west. Cross over the small bridge and under a railroad bridge, then up a hill.

# 3. Oak Creek to North Racine

## *6.9 miles*

*This section is the best available connector route between the
Oak Leaf Bike Path in Milwaukee and the Racine County Bike
Route in Racine County. The 3.3 miles on Highway 32 are trav-
elled strictly to get you from Point A to Point B.*

**ROUTE:** From Oak Creek Parkway until you reach the intersection of
Ryan Road and Chicago Road (Highway 32), you are on quiet roads
through suburbs and industrial areas. On Highway 32, there is no
possible route to the east until you get to 7 Mile Road. Highway 32
has a narrow shoulder. 7 Mile Road is a country road.

**SURFACE:** Paved streets. There are no bike paths of any sort in this
section.

**TRAFFIC:** This is the toughest section of the whole trip. The 3.3 miles
along Highway 32 are busy highway riding. There is a shoulder, but
it is only 2 feet wide. Otherwise, the other roads are quiet to moderate in traffic.

**POINTS OF INTEREST:** Little of interest.

**FACILITIES:** There are tavern/restaurants along 5th Avenue in Oak Creek,
and there are tavern/restaurants along Highway 32. Once you turn
off Highway 32, there are no facilities until you get to Racine.

**SIDE TRIPS:** a) At Oak Creek Parkway, at the start of this route section, you can continue on the Oak Leaf Bike Path, which circles back to downtown Milwaukee in 76 miles.

b) At 7 Mile Road and the Racine Bike Trail at the end of this route section, you can continue east on 7 Mile Road and eventually rejoin this recommended route in the City of Racine.

**ALTERNATIVES:** For a faster option, stay on Highway 32 through Racine. This is fast riding, few stops and traffic.

**OTHER INFORMATION:** The only other information you might want in this section is a good map. The best map that shows all the minor roads that you travel is the Road Map of Southeastern Wisconsin available from:

Milwaukee Map Service Inc.
959 North Mayfair Road
Milwaukee, Wisconsin 53226
(800) 525-3822 or (414) 774-1300

**PARKING:** No long-term parking is available at either end of the route section. There is parking on 5th Avenue in Oak Creek and in parking lots for restaurants on Highway 32. Good parking in parking lots at the corner of Ryan Road and Chicago Road (Highway 32).

**SIDE TRIPS:** None of any interest.

**DIRECTIONS (Mile marker/**Description):
**0.0** Oak Creek Parkway in front of lagoon. South on unmarked street becomes 6th Avenue.

**0.1** Milwaukee Avenue and 6th Avenue, stop sign. Left 1 block to 5th Avenue, which turns south.

**0.2** 5th Avenue, right (south).

**1.4** Road narrows but usually low traffic.

**2.9** Ryan Road (9500S). 5th Avenue ends. Right (west) and cross railroad tracks.

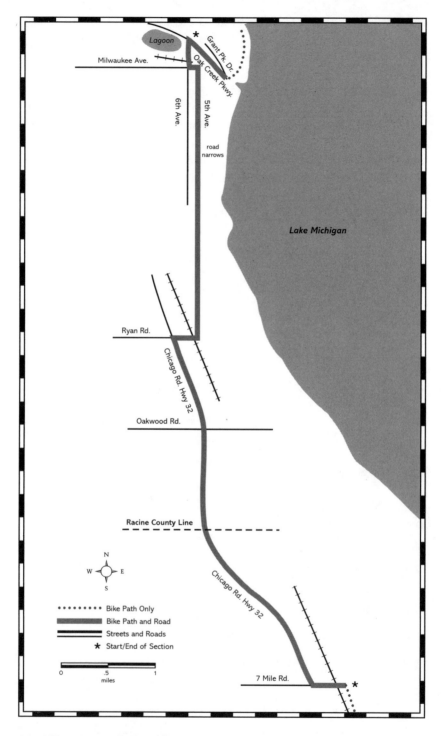

Lagoon

Grant Pk. Dr.

Milwaukee Ave.

Oak Creek Pkwy.

6th Ave.

5th Ave.

road narrows

Lake Michigan

Ryan Rd.

Chicago Rd. Hwy 32

Oakwood Rd.

Racine County Line

N
W — E
S

Chicago Rd. Hwy 32

•••••••• Bike Path Only
Bike Path and Road
Streets and Roads
★ Start/End of Section

0    .5    1
miles

7 Mile Rd.

★

**3.2** Chicago Road (3800 E), (Highway 32 South), stop sign. Left (south), narrow shoulder. Traffic can be heavy on this highway.

**4.2** Cross Oakwood Road.

**5.3** Racine County/Milwaukee County line. Continue on 32 South.

**6.5** 7 Mile Road, left (east) and cross the railroad tracks.

**6.9** Racine County Bicycle Trail, right (south).

# 4. North Racine Bike Path

## *5.8 miles*

*This bike path is on an old rail bed. The scenery is dull, along high electrical wire towers. It is straight and fast. The trail doesn't go through central Racine, so there is a city ride between the north and south portions of the county bike path.*

**ROUTE:** This section is all on an off-street trail. You cross occasional roads that are named after the distance from central Racine. The bike trail is straight and simple to follow. North of 7 Mile Road, the trail is not passable.

**SURFACE:** The trail has a crushed stone surface, which is generally firm and smooth. There is no problem for any kind of bike.

**TRAFFIC:** Very light bike traffic. The cross roads carry moderate traffic.

**POINTS OF INTEREST:** There are no points of interest on the bike trail itself. Side trips will take you to the pretty area of Wind Point or to Cliffside Park.

**FACILITIES:** There are no facilities along this 5.8 mile stretch of bike path. There is a convenience store two blocks east of the bike path on 4 Mile Road.

**SIDE LIGHTS:** None.

**ALTERNATIVES:** You can follow Highway 32 (Chicago Road/Douglas Road into Racine. This is a fast, direct route with traffic. A longer, more scenic route through the suburbs of Racine is available. Continue on 7 Mile Road, take city streets along the lake. This route is longer, more circuitous and more interesting. 7 Mile Road to Michina Road to 6 Mile Road to Novak Road to 5 ½ Mile Road to Charles Road to 4 Mile Road to Erie Street to Main Street (south) or 4 Mile Road to Wind Point to Light House Drive to Michigan Boulevard to Main.

**OTHER INFORMATION:** You can get two different maps of this bike path. Frankly, neither is of any real help. A "Racine County Bicycle and Pedestrian Trails" map is available from:

Racine County Public Works
14200 Washington Avenue
Sturtevant, Wisconsin 53177
(414) 886-8440

Also, a "Racine and Kenosha County Trails" map is available from some bike stores or:

American Bike Trails
1430 Main Street
Suite 525
Des Plaines, Illinois 60616

**PARKING:** There are no parking lots at either end of this trail section, although you can park on the street, but it is not recommended for multiday use.

**SIDE TRIPS:** The alternate route to Wind Point could also be considered a side trip. At 6 Mile Road, Cliffside County Park is to the east. Follow the signs directing you to the park.

**DIRECTIONS (Mile marker/**Description):

**0.0** At 7 Mile Road and the start of the bike path. South.

**1.0** Cross 6 Mile Road (possible side trip to Cliffside County Park.)

**2.1** Cross 5 Mile Road.

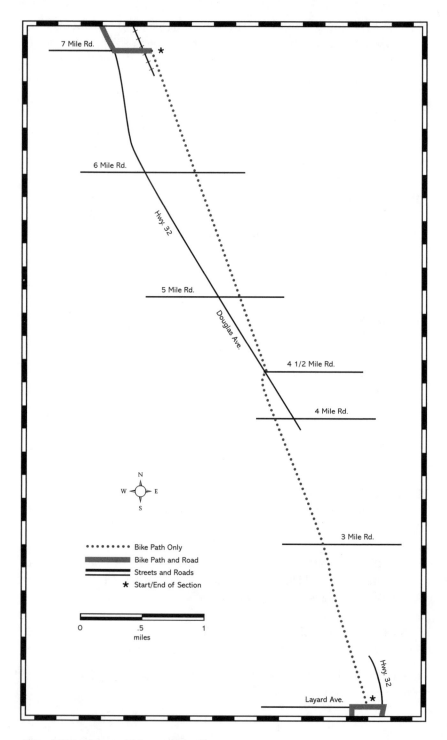

7 Mile Rd.

6 Mile Rd.

Hwy. 32

5 Mile Rd.

Douglas Ave.

4 1/2 Mile Rd.

4 Mile Rd.

N
W ⬥ E
S

3 Mile Rd.

•••••••••• Bike Path Only
Bike Path and Road
Streets and Roads
* Start/End of Section

0          .5          1
miles

Hwy. 32

Layard Ave.

102   **Milwaukee to Chicago (South)**

**2.6** Cross 4 ½ Mile Road and Douglas Avenue, busy intersection. Cross both and ride on Douglas Avenue (Highway 32) for 150 feet (south). Bear right onto the bike path on the right (west side) of Douglas Avenue.

**3.2** Cross 4 Mile Road. Convenience store 2 blocks east of the bike path.

**4.4** Cross 3 Mile Road.

**5.8** Bike path ends at Layard Avenue in Racine.

# 5. Racine

## *4.2 miles or 6.3 miles*

*The Racine County Bike Path does not pass through the City of Racine. The two options are either direct or through downtown Racine.*

**OPTION A:** Downtown Route. 6.3 miles to the bike path on the south side of Racine. Somewhat scenic and of more interest.

**OPTION B:** Direct Route. 4.2 miles to the bike path on the south side of Racine. Fast, little of interest, somewhat unsafe. Be aware that you are near a high crime area.

**ROUTE:** Both routes are all on city streets. The downtown route takes you east to Lake Michigan through downtown Racine and finally west again to the bike path. The direct route is 2.1 miles shorter and faster along wide streets on the west side of the downtown area.

**SURFACE:** The whole route is on paved city streets.

**TRAFFIC:** The downtown route at certain hours can be busy on the main streets. Along Michigan Boulevard it is always quiet. The direct route is on main streets that carry traffic, but they are all four lanes. The quieter route is through downtown.

**POINTS OF INTEREST:** The downtown route is along the lake and near the new downtown boat marina. Downtown Racine has a lot of interesting historical buildings. At 4.6 miles, you pass Johnson Wax.

The Landmark Tower office building was designed by Frank Lloyd Wright. The direct route has little of interest.

**FACILITIES:** Lots of restaurants, convenience stores on both routes.

**SIDE LIGHTS:** On the downtown route at Monument Square (3.0 mile mark) is the Recycles Bike Shop. This bike shop has a big inventory of used bikes with a total value of less than what your bike is worth.

**ALTERNATIVES:** You could continue on Highway 32 through downtown to Durand Avenue and then west to the bike path. Lots of traffic. If you chose the alternate route to Wind Point, eventually you must take Highway 32 since there are no through routes on the north side of Racine.

**OTHER INFORMATION:** Neither the Racine County Bicycle and Pedestrian Trails Map nor the Racine and Kenosha County Trails Map help the cyclist through the city. City maps can be obtained from the Racine County Convention and Visitors Bureau at (800)CRACINE.

**PARKING:** There is parking on the lakefront in Racine for multiday use for the downtown route. For the direct route, you must take care for secure parking. Not recommended.

**SIDE TRIPS:** There are roads east of Main Street, downtown which go out to the boat marina on Lake Michigan.

**DIRECTIONS (Mile marker/**Description):
**DOWNTOWN ROUTE (A)**

**0.0** Bike path at Layard Avenue. East on Layard Avenue 1 ½ blocks.

**0.1** Douglas Avenue (Highway 32). Right (south). (Busy four-lane street.)

**0.2** Goold Street (Highway 32), left (east). Follow Highway 32 east.

**0.9** Cross Highway 32, which turns south; don't turn. Go one more block to...

**1.0** Michigan Boulevard, right (south) along the lake.

**2.0** Michigan Boulevard ends. Turn right (west), then 3 blocks.

**2.2** Main Street, left (south) over new bridge. Go through downtown on a

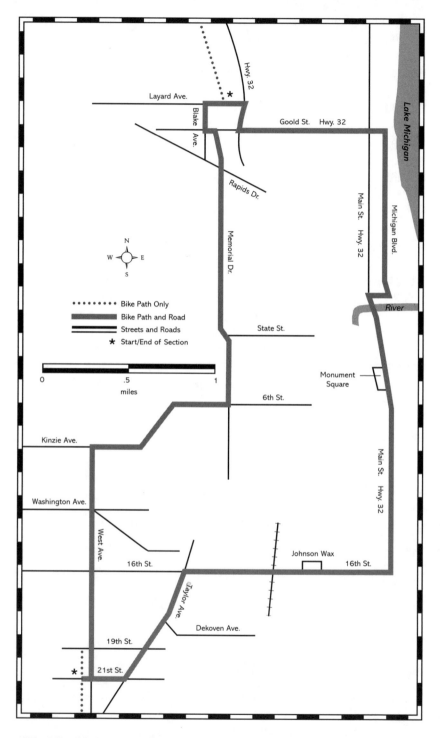

Lake Michigan

Hwy. 32

Layard Ave.

★

Blake Ave.

Goold St.    Hwy. 32

Rapids Dr.

Main St.    Hwy. 32

Michigan Blvd.

Memorial Dr.

N
W — E
S

•••••••••• Bike Path Only
━━━━━━ Bike Path and Road
━━━━━━ Streets and Roads
★ Start/End of Section

0            .5            1
miles

State St.

River

Monument
Square

6th St.

Kinzie Ave.

Main St.    Hwy. 32

Washington Ave.

West Ave.

16th St.

Johnson Wax

16th St.

Taylor Ave.

Dekoven Ave.

19th St.

★

21st St.

4-lane street, busy, especially during the weekdays. 1 block east is a one way north.

**3.0** Monument Square RECYCLES BIKE SHOP.

**3.9** Main Street becomes one way going north. Cross to lake side sidewalk to...

**4.0** 16th Street, then right (west).

**4.6** Johnson Wax. Share the road with traffic.

**4.9** Railroad tracks.

**5.3** Taylor Avenue, left (south).

**5.7** Cross DeKoven Street.

**6.1** 21st Street, right (west).

**6.3** Bike path, left (south). Narrow to begin with.

**DIRECT ROUTE (B)**

**0.0** Layard Avenue, right (west) for 1 block.

**0.1** Blake Avenue, left (south) for 1 block.

**0.2** Goold Street, left (east) for 1 block.

**0.3** Memorial Drive, right (south), 4-lane road.

**0.5** Cross Rapids Drive stop light.

**1.4** Cross State Street; road jogs left, then right.

**1.9** 6th Street, right (west)

**2.2** Over Root River; jog left (south). Becomes Kinzie Avenue.

**2.5** Jog west on Kinzie Avenue.

**2.9** West Avenue, left (south). You follow West Avenue all the way to the bike path.

**3.2** Cross Washington Avenue.

**3.6** Cross 16th Street.

**3.9** Cross 19th Street. On the right is the beginning of the bicycle path running parallel.

**4.2** 21st Street and the bike path.

# 6. Racine County/ Kenosha County Bike Path

## *7.1 miles*

*This bike path runs between south Racine and North Kenosha. This path does not run through either the City of Racine or the City of Kenosha. The scenery along this section is superior to that of the northern section of the Racine County Bike Path.*

**ROUTE:** The bike trail starts at West Avenue and 21st Street in Racine and ends at 35th Street between 30th Avenue and 22nd Avenue in Kenosha. This trail is a rails-to-trails conversion, so it is absolutely straight south/north.

**SURFACE:** The trail is crushed gravel that is well maintained. There are a few soft spots.

**TRAFFIC:** Bike traffic is very light. The cross roads are generally quiet and easy to cross.

**POINTS OF INTEREST:** Nice scenery.

**FACILITIES:** No water or bathrooms on the trail. At 5.8 miles, there is the Glenwood Crossings Shopping Center 3 blocks west of the trail.

**SIDE LIGHTS:** The Kenosha Country Club.

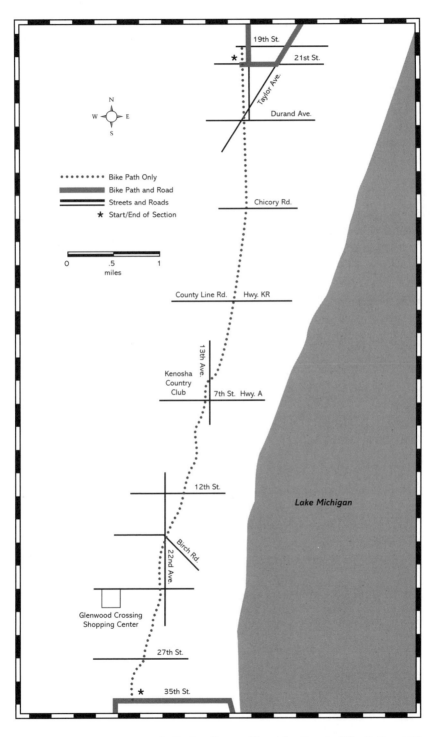

19th St.

★ 21st St.

Taylor Ave.

Durand Ave.

········· Bike Path Only

Bike Path and Road

Streets and Roads

★ Start/End of Section

Chicory Rd.

N
W E
S

0    .5    1
miles

County Line Rd.    Hwy. KR

13th Ave.

Kenosha
Country
Club        7th St.  Hwy. A

12th St.

Lake Michigan

Birch Rd.

22nd Ave.

Glenwood Crossing
Shopping Center

27th St.

★ 35th St.

**6. Racine County/Kenosha County Bike Path**  109

**ALTERNATIVES:** Highway 32 runs along Lake Michigan east of the bike path. There is traffic. You have to pick up the highway in the City of Racine and end in the City of Kenosha.

**OTHER INFORMATION:** A "Racine and Kenosha County Trails" map is available from some bike stores or:

American Bike Trails
1430 Main Street
Suite 525
Des Plaines, Illinois 60016

**PARKING:** Multiday parking at the north trailhead is not recommended. At the south end of this trail, there is street parking in suburban areas. This parking is safe, even for multiple days.

**SIDE TRIPS:** The "Racine County Bicycle and Pedestrian Trails" map and the "Racine and Kenosha County Trails" map show road routes to the west toward Burlington.

**DIRECTIONS (Mile marker/**Description):
**0.0**  Bike path at 21st Street. Crushed stone path. South.

**0.5**  Cross Durand Avenue.

**1.5**  Cross road.

**2.6**  Cross roads. Nice scenery, first suburbs, then country farms.

**3.3**  Kenosha Country Club. Cross road.

**3.7**  Cross road.

**4.7**  Cross 12th Street.

**5.2**  Cross both Birch Road and 22nd Avenue and continue on path.

**5.8**  Cross roads. Glenwood Crossing Shopping Center to west on road.

**6.6**  Cross 27th Street.

**7.1**  End of trail. Sign states 9.4 miles for bike path.

# 7. Kenosha

## *4.5 miles or 8.4 miles*

*Once again, you are between trails. However, the scenic route through Kenosha is a very enjoyable ride and recommended.*

**OPTION A:** Direct Route. Fastest route of limited interest. This route is virtually straight south along a wide road. 4.5 miles.

**OPTION B:** Scenic Route. Much slower but very interesting along the lakefront and through downtown. 8.4 miles.

**ROUTE:** The direct route is straight along 30th Avenue. This is absolutely the shortest route. The scenic route takes you east to Lake Michigan, south along the lake and then back west again to the trail. This route is pretty well marked and incorporates some bike trails through lakeside parks.

**SURFACE:** All on city streets except for the paved bike paths along the lake through the parks.

**TRAFFIC:** All the roads on both routes are quiet to moderately busy, depending on the time of day. Obviously, in the downtown area on the scenic route, there is heavier traffic on 6th Avenue.

**POINTS OF INTEREST:** On the direct route you pass the Chrysler Engine Plant, which at one time employed 5,000 but now employs 1,000. On the scenic route, you see the new boat marina, downtown Kenosha and excellent views of Lake Michigan.

**FACILITIES:** Plenty of restaurants and stores along both routes.

**SIDE LIGHTS:** The huge open space east of downtown is where the old Chrysler Plant once stood. This was the heart of the Kenosha economy, but the community has found a way to prosper without it. Also on the scenic route, at 3.8 miles, you pass Kemper Hall, which is a former women's prep school. Also at 7.1 miles you pass the Keno Drive-In Theatre. One of the very last of a disappearing venue.

**ALTERNATIVES:** There are many options, but these are the two best. Any city streets south will eventually get you to the south bike path.

**OTHER INFORMATION:** The "Racine and Kenosha County Trails" map has a very generalized guide through the scenic route but is really of little value.

**PARKING:** At either end of this route section, street parking is available. It is safe and multiday use should be fine.

**SIDE TRIPS:** Out around the boat marina east of downtown.

**DIRECTIONS (Mile marker/**Description):
**DIRECT ROUTE (A)**

**0.0** Trail ends at 35th Street. 35th Street west for 2 blocks to 30th Avenue.

**0.1** 30th Avenue, left (south) on a 4-lane road with traffic. Urban ride.

**1.5** Pass Chrysler Engine Plant.

**3.0** Cross 76th Street. (Total Cyclery Bicycle Shop is just east on 76th Street off 35th Street.)

**3.5** Cross Snap-On Drive.

**4.5** Cross 89th Street. Start of bike path (3.5 miles to the state line).

**SCENIC ROUTE (B)**

**0.0** 35th Street, end of bike trail. East on 35th Street.

**0.3** Cross 22nd Avenue. Bike route signs start. Follow signs.

**1.0** Cross Sheridan Road.

**1.1** Cross 7th Avenue. Cross and bear right (south) on bike path through

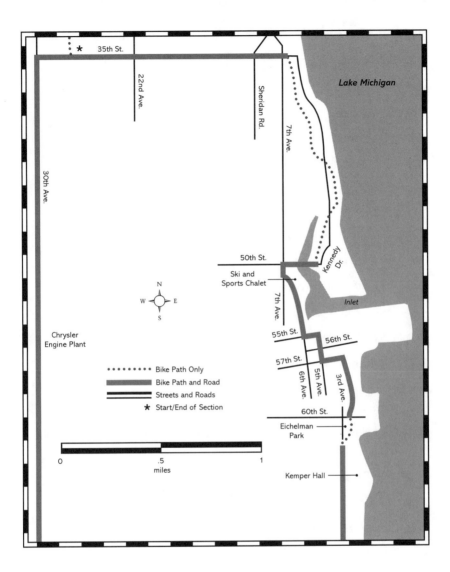

parks. Follow the bike route signs.

**1.9** Cross street to shoreline.

**2.2** Cross back over street on bike path.

**2.3** Kennedy Drive and 50th Street. Bike path ends. Right (west) on 50th Street.

**2.4** Bridge over harbor.

**2.5** 7th Avenue, left (south). 7th Avenue angles into 6th Avenue (south).

**2.6** Ski and Sports Chalet (bike shop).

**2.8** 55th Street, left (east) to...

**2.9** 5th Avenue, right (south) to...

**3.0** 57th Street, left (east) to...

**3.1** 3rd Avenue, right (south).

**3.4** Cross 60th Street, straight (south) onto bike path through Eichelman Park and continue south.

**3.6** 3rd Avenue, left (south).

**3.8** Kemper Hall. Follow bike signs.

**4.2** 69th Street, left (east).

**4.2** 2nd Avenue, right (south).

**4.3** 71st Street, left (east).

**4.4** 1st Avenue, right (south).

**4.6** Cross 75th Street, continue straight south onto bike trail along lake shore in Southport Park to 78th Street.

**4.9** Stop sign. Path swings west and ends. Follow road that swings right (little north and west) and ends on 78th Street and 3rd Avenue.

**5.0** 78th Street, left (west).

**5.3** 7th Avenue, left (south); 78th Street ends. Follow signs.

**5.5** Cross 80th Street, 7th Avenue narrows, low traffic.

**6.8** 7th Avenue swings west and becomes 91st Street.

**6.8** Railroad tracks.

**7.1** Cross Sheridan Road (Highway 32), straight on 91st Street. Keno Drive-In Theatre.

**7.6** Highway ML, right (north). Also 22nd Avenue. 2 blocks.

**7.9** 89th Street, left (west) on bike path on north side of street along Anderson Park.

**8.4** Bike path to south at corner of 89th Street and 30th Avenue.

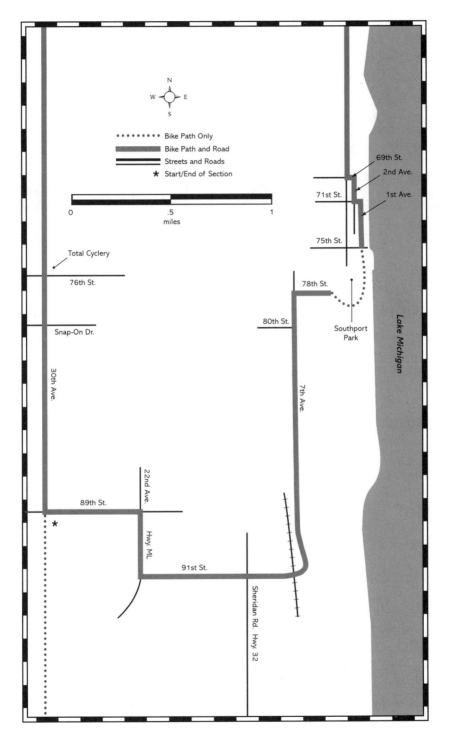

Bike Path Only
Bike Path and Road
Streets and Roads
★ Start/End of Section

N
W E
S

0 .5 1
miles

69th St.
2nd Ave.
71st St.
1st Ave.
75th St.

Total Cyclery

76th St.

Snap-On Dr.

30th Ave.

22nd Ave.

89th St.

Hwy. ML

91st St.

78th St.

80th St.

7th Ave.

Southport Park

Lake Michigan

Sheridan Rd. Hwy. 32

# 8. Kenosha County Bike Path South

## 3.5 miles

*This path, starting on the south side of Kenosha, goes 3.5 miles to the Illinois/Wisconsin state line but is the start of a 23.5 mile continuous series of bike paths that finally ends at Fort Sheridan in Highwood.*

**ROUTE:** From 30th Avenue and 89th Street on the southwest side of the City of Kenosha to the state line. Straight south.

**SURFACE:** The Kenosha County Bike Path is crushed gravel. The path is a little soft in areas.

**TRAFFIC:** Light bike use with few cross roads.

**POINTS OF INTEREST:** The Illinois/Wisconsin state line at Russell Road.

**FACILITIES:** None.

**SIDE LIGHTS:** It is very easy to miss the transition to the bike path in Illinois.

**ALTERNATIVES:** It is possible to continue to ride south along Lake Michigan to 116th Street on 1st Avenue and then take 116th Street west to the bike path.

**OTHER INFORMATION:** The "Racine and Kenosha County Trails" map.

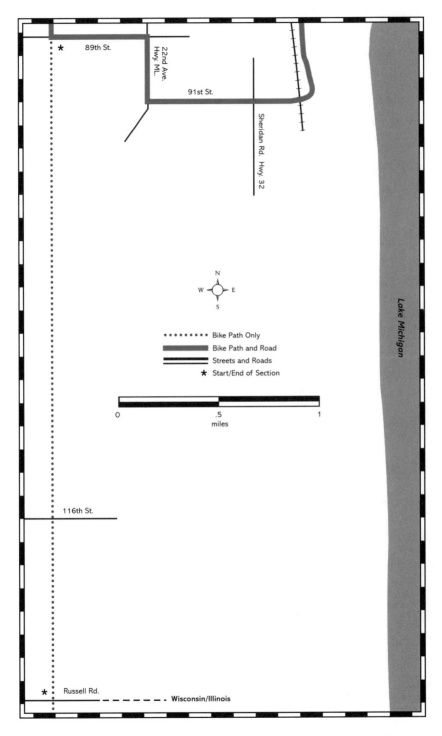

89th St.

22nd Ave. Hwy. ML.

91st St.

Sheridan Rd. Hwy. 32

Lake Michigan

N
W ⊙ E
S

•••••••• Bike Path Only
▬▬▬ Bike Path and Road
═══ Streets and Roads
★ Start/End of Section

0          .5          1
        miles

116th St.

Russell Rd.
———————— Wisconsin/Illinois

**8. Kenosha County Bike Path South** 117

**PARKING:** There is no parking at the state line. The path goes over Russell Road on a bridge. There is safe street parking at the start of this bike trail, even for multiple days.

**SIDE TRIPS:** None.

**DIRECTIONS (Mile marker/**Description):

**0.0** 30th Avenue and 89th Street, south side of Kenosha. Bike Path south.

**2.5** Cross 116th Street (unmarked).

**3.5** Over bridge at Russell Road; Illinois state line.

# 9. Lake County Bike Path North

## 2.5 miles

*This section of the continuous off-road bike path starts at the state line and ends in Zion, where the path continues but is maintained by the City of Zion. There are mileage markers every .5 mile.*

**ROUTE:** At the state line, the path continues and goes over a bridge at Russell Road. The path is a continuation of the Kenosha route along the same old railroad bed. It ends at 21st Street and Galilee Avenue in Zion.

**SURFACE:** This is a crushed gravel path. It is the same surface as in Kenosha.

**TRAFFIC:** The bike traffic is very light at all times.

**POINTS OF INTEREST:** The Illinois/Wisconsin state line.

**FACILITIES:** None, not even off the trail.

**SIDE LIGHTS:** The rails-to-trails proceeds along the same line whether in Kenosha or Lake County.

**ALTERNATIVES:** There are road options to the east or west of the trail but not worth the effort.

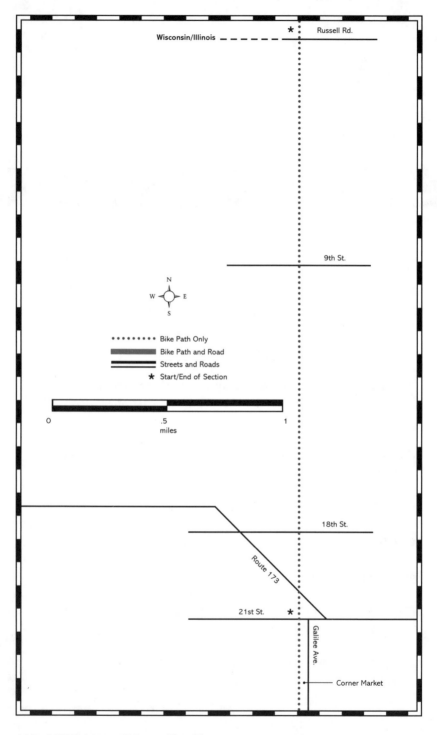

**OTHER INFORMATION:** A section of *Hiking and Biking in Lake County, Illinois* by Jim Hochgesang describes this route and other interconnected routes in Lake County.

**PARKING:** There is plenty of parking but on the streets.

**SIDE TRIPS:** Near 17th Street, at the top of a hill, follow the bike path sign right (east) on Ravine Drive. The route is on the street until 18th Street and Gideon Streets, where a trail (paved) to Illinois State Park starts.

**DIRECTIONS (Mile marker/**Description):

**0.0** North Shore Path of Lake County at Russell Road (state line) south.

**1.0** Cross 9th Street.

**2.2** Cross 18th Street.

**2.4** Cross bridge over Route 173.

**2.5** End of path at 21st Street and Galilee Avenue.

# 10. Zion Bike Path

## *1.5 miles*

*This is a connector route between the north and south sections of the Lake County Bike Path.*

**ROUTE:** 21st Street to Carmel Avenue along Galilee Avenue in Zion.

**SURFACE:** The off-road bike path is paved.

**TRAFFIC:** Very light bike traffic.

**POINTS OF INTEREST:** None.

**FACILITIES:** A market for food and drinks .6 miles from 21st Street on east side of Galilee Avenue.

**SIDE LIGHTS:** None.

**ALTERNATIVES:** If preferred, you can ride on Galilee Avenue, which has moderate traffic and is wide.

**OTHER INFORMATION:** A section of *Hiking and Biking in Lake County, Illinois* by Jim Hochgesang describes this route and other interconnected routes in Lake County.

**PARKING:** There is street parking along Galilee Avenue.

**SIDE TRIPS:** To Illinois Beach State Park North Unit (start is in previous

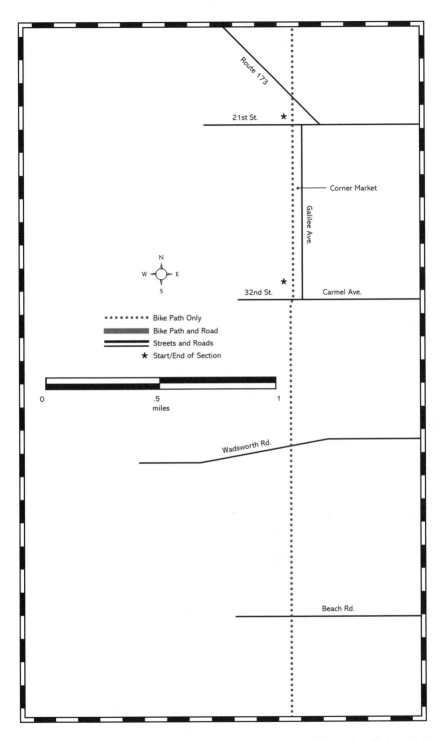

Route 173

21st St. ★

Corner Market

Galilee Ave.

32nd St. ★

Carmel Ave.

N
W ⊕ E
S

•••••••• Bike Path Only
�largeshade Bike Path and Road
━━━ Streets and Roads
★ Start/End of Section

0                    .5                    1
                    miles

Wadsworth Rd.

Beach Rd.

**10. Zion Bike Path** 123

chapter) then south in park past the Power House to the South Unit of the Park and west again on Carmel Avenue to the intersection of the Zion and North Shore Bike Paths. 6.3 mile loop.

**DIRECTIONS (Mile marker/**Description):

**0.0** 21st Street and Galilee Avenue. Straight (south) on bike/walking path on the west side of Galilee Avenue.

**0.6** Corner market. Now going through Zion.

**1.5** Bear right at Y in the path. Left is paved, right is gravel. North Shore path starts again at Carmel Avenue.

# 11. Lake County Bike Path South

## *9.7 miles*

*This section is all on dedicated bike trail. The trail begins at Carmel Avenue in Zion and ends just south of the main entrance to Great Lakes Naval Station just west of Sheridan Road. This path, called the North Shore Path, was built on the old North Shore Railway right of way and runs north and south straight through Waukegan and North Chicago in Lake County.*

**ROUTE:** Because it follows the old rail right of way, it is straight. Through the urban communities of Waukegan and North Chicago, there are numerous street crossings. The route is adjacent to busy streets between 8 and 9 miles into this route section. The route directions are complex, but the signage is very good. Under the underpass, watch for broken glass and debris.

**SURFACE:** The northern part of this section has a well maintained crushed gravel surface. The part along Sheridan Road is paved. This section ends where the cement bike/walking path becomes an asphalt path. (Green Bay Trail.)

**TRAFFIC:** Throughout this section, the bike and walking traffic is light to moderate. Because of the numerous cross streets, however, your progress will be slowed.

**POINTS OF INTEREST:** Great Lakes Naval Training Station, which covers

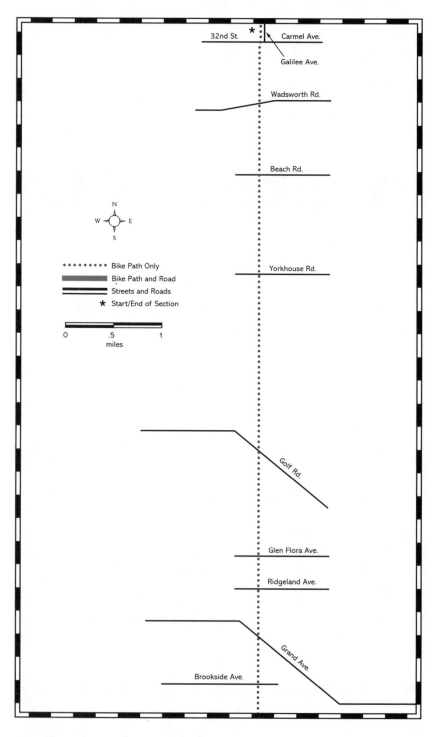

32nd St. ⭐ Carmel Ave.

Galilee Ave.

Wadsworth Rd.

Beach Rd.

N
W ⟡ E
S

Yorkhouse Rd.

•••••••••• Bike Path Only
▬▬▬▬ Bike Path and Road
▬▬▬▬ Streets and Roads
⭐ Start/End of Section

0       .5       1
miles

Golf Rd.

Glen Flora Ave.

Ridgeland Ave.

Grand Ave.

Brookside Ave.

1,628 acres and trains 30,000 recruits annually, employs over 9,000 military and 3,500 civilian employees.

**FACILITIES:** In spite of being in urban surroundings, there are no water fountains or restrooms. Restaurants and stoies are available. At Washington Street there is a bakery.

**SIDE LIGHTS:** None.

**ALTERNATIVES:** City streets are available, especially through Waukegan. Also, depending on your tolerance level for traffic, Highway 32 is a fast, straight alternative.

**OTHER INFORMATION:** A section of *Hiking and Biking in Lake County, Illinois* by Jim Hochgesang describes this route and other interconnected routes in Lake County.

Also, a cartoonlike map of Lake County that does not show the bike path is available from:

The Lake County Convention & Visitors Bureau
401 North Riverside Drive, Suite 5
Gurnee, Illinois 60031-5906
(847) 662-2700, (800) 525-3669 or
FAX (847) 662-2702

**PARKING:** There is plenty of day parking on the streets along this route. A good parking lot for day use and multiple day use is at the train station for Great Lakes near Farragut Avenue on Sheridan Road.

**SIDE TRIPS:** Take Carmel Boulevard east, then east on 32nd Street to Elisha Avenue, south to 33rd Street, east to Sheridan Road, north for ½ block to the corner of Sheridan Road and Carmel Boulevard, where the Illinois Beach State Park path commences on the right.

**DIRECTIONS (Mile marker/**Description):
**0.0** North Shore path begins at Carmel Avenue in Zion. South.

**0.5** Over bridge at Wadsworth Road.

**1.2** Cross Beach Road.

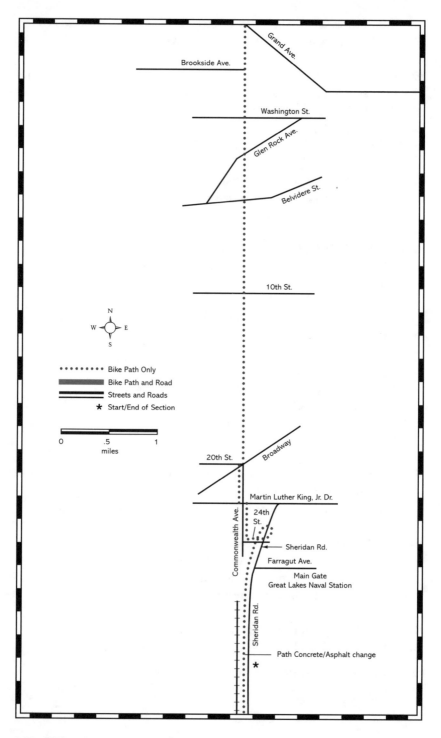

Grand Ave.

Brookside Ave.

Washington St.

Glen Rock Ave.

Belvidere St.

10th St.

N
W ⊕ E
S

•••••••• Bike Path Only
▬▬▬▬ Bike Path and Road
▬▬▬▬ Streets and Roads
★ Start/End of Section

0        .5        1
miles

20th St.          Broadway

Martin Luther King, Jr. Dr.

Commonwealth Ave.

24th
St.

Sheridan Rd.

Farragut Ave.

Main Gate
Great Lakes Naval Station

Sheridan Rd.

Path Concrete/Asphalt change

★

**2.0**  Cross York House Road.

**3.4**  Cross Golf Road. Now going west of Waukegan; many cross roads.

**4.3**  Cross Glen Flora Avenue.

**4.5**  Cross Ridgeland Avenue.

**4.8**  Cross Grand Avenue.

**5.2**  Cross Brookside Avenue.

**5.5**  Cross Washington Street. (Bakery to left.)

**5.8**  Cross Glen Rock Avenue.

**6.1**  Cross Belvidere Street.

**6.8**  Cross 10th Street.

**8.1**  Cross Broadway Avenue. Start of paved path adjacent to Commonwealth Avenue. Cross over to left side of Commonwealth Avenue at Martin Luther King, Jr., Drive.

**8.6**  24th Street. Bear left (east). (Path is well marked.)

**8.7**  Under underpass on left side of 24th Street. Circle back and around. Watch for broken glass and debris.

**8.8**  Sheridan Road. Cross to west side and follow North Shore Path signs. South.

**9.1**  Farragut Avenue. Opposite the main gate to Great Lakes Naval Station. Cement path on west side of Sheridan Road.

**9.7**  End of North Shore Path of Lake County. At point where cement path becomes an asphalt path.

# 12. North Shore Bike Path North

## *6.3 miles*

*This is the last section of the continuous bike path from Kenosha, Wisconsin. The start of this section is opposite Great Lakes Naval Station, 0.6 miles south of the main entrance on Sheridan Road. This is the point where the North Shore Path becomes the Green Bay Trail. The path changes from asphalt to cement. You pass through Lake Forest and Lake Bluff. The path ends at Old Elm Road just north of Highwood.*

**ROUTE:** Generally, the route runs between the navy and the army, from Great Lakes Naval Station to Fort Sheridan. The off-road path runs alongside Sheridan Road on the east and the Metra Railroad Tracks on the west. In Lake Forest, you pass through the railroad station parking lot, which connects the path north and south. There is a bike route sign in Lake Forest. Don't follow it. Stay south through the railroad station parking lot.

**SURFACE:** This section of the bike path is asphalt. There is a short connector section through the railroad station parking lot in Lake Forest.

**TRAFFIC:** There is moderate bike traffic on this section. There are few cross roads, some crossed by bridges. Take care through the parking lot.

**POINTS OF INTEREST:** The pleasant village of Lake Bluff and the suburban downtown shopping area of Lake Forest.

**FACILITIES:** Plenty of restaurants and stores in Lake Bluff and Lake Forest.

**SIDE LIGHTS:** An interesting tour of Lake Forest will show you Chicago's most affluent suburb.

**ALTERNATIVES:** Side roads through Lake Bluff and Lake Forest east of the bike path can be explored and used to proceed toward Chicago. A local map will be needed.

**OTHER INFORMATION:** A section of *Hiking and Biking in Lake County, Illinois* by Jim Hochgesang describes this route and other interconnected routes in Lake County.

**PARKING:** There is good parking in the train station parking lots for Lake Forest, Lake Bluff and Great Lakes. There is no parking lot at Old Elm Road, but there are restaurant parking lots just south on Sheridan Road.

**SIDE TRIPS:** Just wander around east of the trail in Lake Bluff and especially Lake Forest. In Lake Forest, go east to Lake Michigan where there is a public beach.

**DIRECTIONS (Mile marker/**Description):

**0.0** Bike path opposite Great Lakes Naval Station alongside of Sheridan Road. Continue south on asphalt path which was concrete.

**1.6** Fork in path, straight. (Right is to the parking lot for the train station for Lake Bluff.)

**1.7** Downtown Lake Bluff is on the left. Path continues on along Sheridan Road.

**3.3** Over the bridge at Woodland Avenue, down to stop sign into a parking lot for the Lake Forest Train Station. Continue through the parking lot (south).

**3.6** Straight through the parking lot. Do not follow the bike route sign.

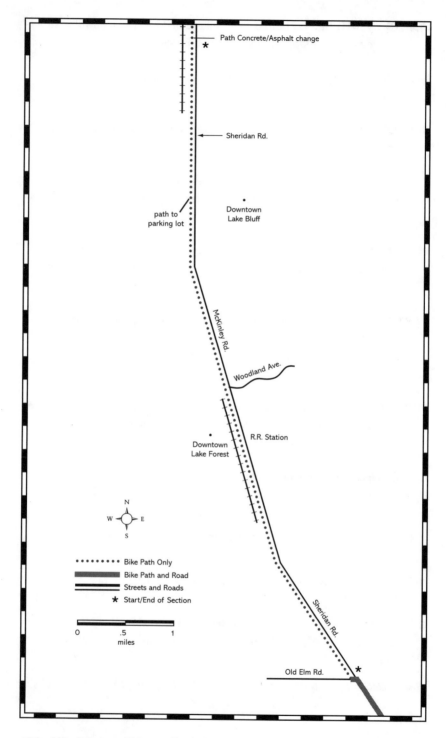

Path Concrete/Asphalt change

Sheridan Rd.

Downtown
Lake Bluff

path to
parking lot

McKinley Rd.

Woodland Ave.

R.R. Station

Downtown
Lake Forest

N
W ✦ E
S

•••••••• Bike Path Only
▬▬▬▬ Bike Path and Road
▬▬▬▬ Streets and Roads
★ Start/End of Section

0        .5        1
   miles

Sheridan Rd.

Old Elm Rd.

**3.7** Downtown Lake Forest (all facilities) is on the right.

**3.8** Straight out of south end of parking lot; go over a bridge. Go along the Metra railroad tracks.

**5.8** Beginning of Fort Sheridan. Straight.

**6.3** Old Elm Road, left (east) for 50 feet, end of the bike path. Go to stop light at Sheridan Road. Right on Sheridan Road (south). Parking.

# 13. Highwood Connector Route

## 1.5 miles

*All of this section is on a busy street. You use this section strictly to connect the bike trails on either side. Sheridan Road is two lanes with some room for bikes but no designated lane. It is possible to ride on a bumpy sidewalk on the east side of the road.*

**ROUTE:** Through Highwood along Sheridan Road straight south. Sheridan Road becomes Waukegan Avenue in downtown Highwood.

**SURFACE:** All on highway with a curb.

**TRAFFIC:** This road is heavily used and is consistently the busiest section of the whole bike route.

**POINTS OF INTEREST:** Fort Sheridan is on a beautiful parcel of land along Lake Michigan. It has been closed and should be developed.

**FACILITIES:** Just south of Old Elm Road, there are fast-food restaurants and convenience stores. In downtown Highwood, there are many restaurants.

**SIDE LIGHTS:** Highwood is a military town.

**ALTERNATIVES:** I wish there were some.

**OTHER INFORMATION:** Really, no other information is necessary.

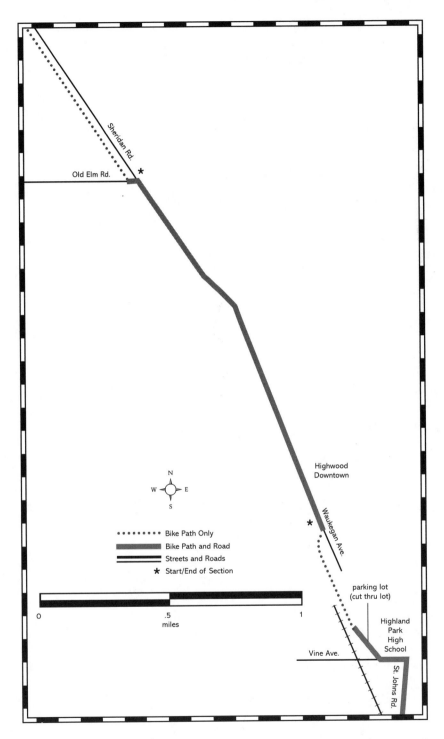

Sheridan Rd.

Old Elm Rd.

*

Highwood
Downtown

Waukegan Ave.

*

N
W ● E
S

●●●●●●●●● Bike Path Only
━━━━━━━ Bike Path and Road
━━━━━━━ Streets and Roads
★ Start/End of Section

0                    .5                    1
                  miles

parking lot
(cut thru lot)

Highland
Park
High
School

Vine Ave.

St. Johns Rd.

**13. Highwood Connector Route** 135

**PARKING:** Street parking is possible in downtown Highwood, but not north of town on the highway. You could park at the fast-food restaurants near Old Elm Road.

**SIDE TRIPS:** None.

**DIRECTIONS (Mile marker/**Description):

**0.0** Old Elm Road, left (east) for 50 feet. (End of bike trail.)

**0.0** Sheridan Road, right (south). Busy two-lane road.

**1.3** Straight through downtown Highwood. Sheridan Road becomes Waukegan Avenue. Same road.

**1.5** Stop sign. Bear right (south) over curb onto the bike path (crushed gravel).

# 14. Lake Shore Bike Path South

## *11.1 miles*

*This is the longest segment of the full trip. This is one of the sections that inspired this guide since it is very easy to lose the way and involves a lot of connections between sections of off-road bike path. When you are on the trails, you can relax but in between, you have to be conscious of these directions.*

**ROUTE:** This route involves lots of connections between bike paths but generally follows the Metra Railroad tracks. The road that generally runs parallel is Green Bay Road, but this is not always the case. Even the local bike riders are confused in this section. This route starts in Highwood and ends at the Wilmette/Evanston boundary.

**SURFACE:** The bike paths are sometimes paved and at other times gravel or dirt. All of the roads and parking lots are paved.

**TRAFFIC:** On the bike trails in some areas the bike, walking or rollerblade traffic can be moderately heavy, especially on the weekends. All the connector roads are pretty quiet. Take care through the parking lots since cars can be backing out of parking places.

**POINTS OF INTEREST:** There are many since you are pedaling through the picturesque North Shore suburbs of Chicago. You pass through Highland Park, Ravinia, Glencoe, Winnetka, Kenilworth and Wilmette. The route goes through all of the business districts.

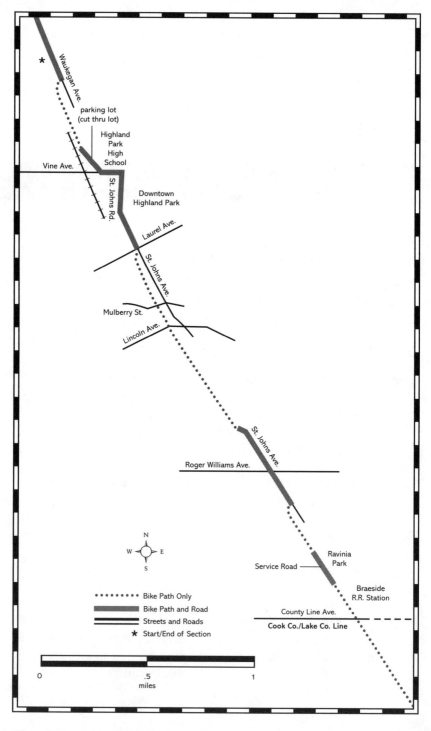

Waukegan Ave.

*

parking lot
(cut thru lot)

Highland
Park
High
School

Vine Ave.

St. Johns Rd.

Downtown
Highland Park

Laurel Ave.

St. Johns Ave.

Mulberry St.

Lincoln Ave.

St. Johns Ave.

Roger Williams Ave.

N
W   E
S

Ravinia
Park

Service Road

Braeside
R.R. Station

County Line Ave.

Cook Co./Lake Co. Line

••••••••• Bike Path Only

Bike Path and Road

Streets and Roads

* Start/End of Section

0       .5       1
miles

**FACILITIES:** There are all types of stores and restaurants in all of these business districts. There is an occasional water fountain in the parks.

**SIDE LIGHTS:** Ravinia Park. This route literally takes you past the main gate. There are concerts (including the Chicago Symphony Orchestra) all summer long in an outside venue.

**ALTERNATIVES:** Using a good local map, you will find street routes available through all these suburbs east of this route. If speed is your intention, you can continue on St. John's Avenue (a busy 2-lane road) at Laurel Avenue (1.2 miles) to County Line Road (3.9 miles) instead of getting back onto the bike path.

**OTHER INFORMATION:** A section of *Hiking and Biking in Cook County, Illinois* by Hochgesang describes this route and other interconnected routes in Cook County.

**PARKING:** There is plenty of parking in all the train station parking lots, but be careful of parking limits and restrictions. On weekends, I've had no problems, even for multiday use.

**SIDE TRIPS:** Here is a side trip that you can devote an additional day to: a trip to the Chicago Botanical Garden. From the Botanical Garden at Lake Cook Road in Glencoe, there is a 19.1 mile asphalt bike trail along the Skokie Lagoons and the Chicago River to Caldwell and Devon Avenues on the north side of Chicago. To get to the Botanical Gardens, at County Line Avenue (3.9 miles), go west on the sidewalk on the north side of Lake Cook Road. (County Line Avenue is Lake Cook Road toward the west.) It is 0.6 miles to the main entrance. Bikes are not allowed on the garden trails, but there are bike racks near the entrance.

**DIRECTIONS (Mile marker/**Description):

**0.0** Bike Path South just south of Highwood on west side of Waukegan Avenue (crushed gravel).

**0.4** Bear left (southeast), cut through parking lot of Highland Park High School to stop sign before street.

**0.5** Vine Avenue, left (east) for 1 ½ blocks. Not marked.

**0.6** St. John's Avenue, right (south). No bike route signs, two lanes.

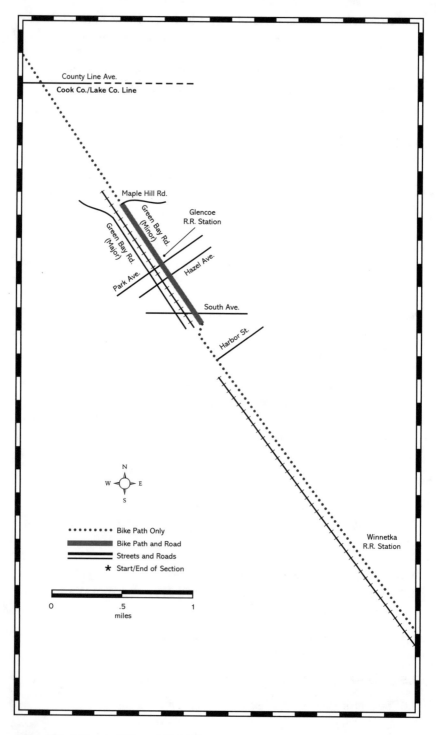

County Line Ave.
Cook Co./Lake Co. Line

Maple Hill Rd.

Green Bay Rd. (Minor)

Green Bay Rd. (Major)

Glencoe R.R. Station

Park Ave.

Hazel Ave.

South Ave.

Harbor St.

N
W · E
S

Winnetka R.R. Station

········· Bike Path Only

▬▬▬▬ Bike Path and Road

══════ Streets and Roads

★ Start/End of Section

0          .5          1
miles

**1.1** Through downtown Highland Park, all facilities. Cross Central Avenue.

**1.2** Laurel Avenue (stop light). Bear right (south) through parking lot on short connector path. Go through the parking lot of the Highland Park Railroad Station.

**1.5** Bear left (south) out of the south end of the parking lot over a bridge and onto the bike path (south). Gravel.

**2.7** Straight into the parking lot of the railroad station. Bear left (east) then right (south) on St. Johns Avenue and cross Roger Williams Avenue.

**2.9** Go onto the sidewalk (south). Bear right onto the gravel bike path.

**3.3** Straight onto the small, paved service road to Ravinia Park (south).

**3.5** Ravinia Park entrance.

**3.6** Straight onto the gravel bike path (south).

**3.8** Straight into the parking lot for Braeside railroad station.

**3.9** Cross County Line Avenue. Back on gravel path marked "Glencoe Greenbay Trail". Cook County/Lake County boundary.

**4.8** Green Bay Road, straight (south) at Maple Hill Road. It is a quiet road on the east side of the railroad tracks. The main Green Bay Road is on the west side of the railroad tracks.

**5.3** Pass by the Glencoe Train Station. Cross Park Avenue. Bear left onto sidewalk (south). Follow bike route sign.

**5.5** Stop sign on fence. Bear right, across the road onto the paved bike path. Short connector path; straight (south) onto road. Again Green Bay Road (minor).

**5.7** Cross South Avenue; straight onto sidewalk for 200 feet and onto the gravel bike path again. The path is narrow and overgrown.

**6.0** Bear left (south) onto paved route through the park. Stay near the railroad tracks.

**6.2** Cross Harbor Street and turn onto the bike path (paved) adjacent to the railroad tracks (south).

**7.9** Pass Winnetka Station.

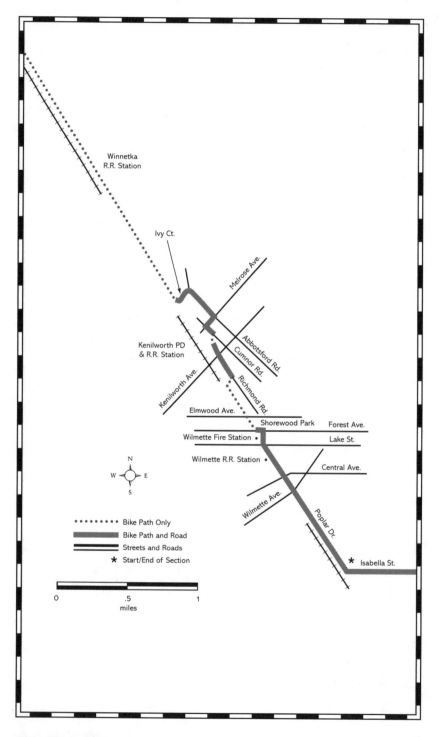

Winnetka
R.R. Station

Ivy Ct.

Melrose Ave.

Abbotsford Rd.

Kenilworth PD
& R.R. Station

Cumnor Rd.

Kenilworth Ave.

Richmond Rd.

Elmwood Ave.

Shorewood Park

Forest Ave.

Wilmette Fire Station

Lake St.

Wilmette R.R. Station

Central Ave.

Wilmette Ave.

Poplar Dr.

N
W · E
S

Isabella St.

• • • • • • •   Bike Path Only

━━━━━   Bike Path and Road

━━━━━   Streets and Roads

✱   Start/End of Section

0        .5        1
miles

**9.1** Sharp left and backtrack (north) 50 feet (bike path ends). Follow bike route signs.

**9.1** Ivy Court, right (east) for 1 block.

**9.2** Abbotsford Road, right (south); quiet suburban road.

**9.4** Melrose Avenue, right (west) 1 block.

**9.5** Cumnor Road, left (south) for 50 feet; then...

**9.5** Right onto bike path through a park onto a paved path (follow signs).

**9.6** Straight onto the road at stop sign, past the Kenilworth police station and train station; past Kenilworth Avenue. Continue on Richmond Road for 100 feet. Bear right onto the bike path (follow sign). A gravel path to a paved path (south) adjacent to the railroad tracks.

**10.0** Across a brick road (Elmwood Avenue).

**10.1** Forest Avenue (next cross road), left (east) for 100 feet. Right (south) past a "Do Not Enter Except for Authorized Vehicles" sign. Disregard the sign; into a parking lot past the Wilmette Fire Station 1.

**10.3** Cross Lake Street and continue through the parking lot for Wilmette Railroad Station.

**10.4** Cross Central Avenue, straight into parking lot. Disregard "No Outlet" sign. Downtown Wilmette.

**10.5** Cross Wilmette Avenue; take Poplar Drive south (the minor road just to the left of the railroad tracks).

**11.1** Isabella Street, left (east) in Evanston.

# 15. Evanston

## 5.3 miles

*There is a good route through Evanston. This route follows a recommended route taken from the excellent Evanston Bikeways Map. It is generally on quiet streets and interconnects with the bike paths through the Northwestern University Campus. Finally, this route takes you to the City of Chicago at Lake Michigan.*

**ROUTE:** Starting at the boundary of Wilmette and Evanston at Isabella Street and Poplar Drive, you finally deviate from the Metra tracks and cross eastward to Lake Michigan. You enter Chicago on the lakefront.

**SURFACE:** The bike paths through Northwestern University campus are paved. If chosen, some of the bike paths south of the campus are gravel but most are asphalt. Before the campus, the route is on city streets.

**TRAFFIC:** On nice days, the nonvehicular traffic on the bike paths can be heavy. The on-road portion of the route is on quiet to moderately trafficked roads.

**POINTS OF INTEREST:** The Northwestern University Campus on Lake Michigan. There are various routes through the campus, with the ones farthest east affording exciting views of the Chicago Loop along the lake.

**FACILITIES:** This particular route doesn't pass any stores or restaurants.

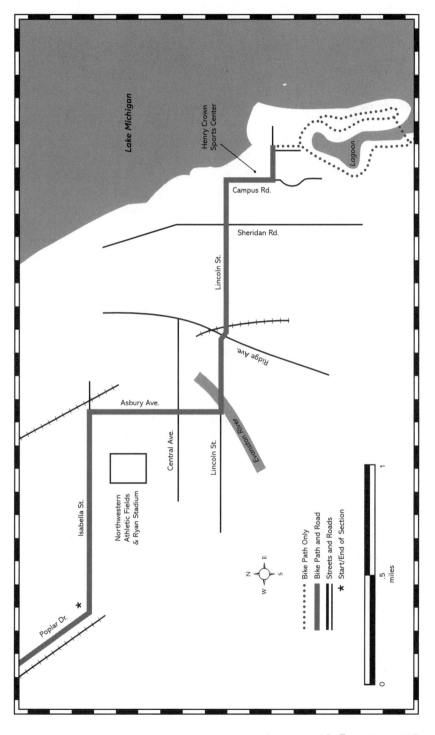

There are drinking fountains and bathrooms in the City of Evanston parks at the lakefront.

**SIDE LIGHTS**: The Northwestern University athletic fields and Ryan Stadium. If timed right, on a Saturday afternoon in the fall, you can avoid the hassles of driving and parking and catch a Wildcat football game.

**ALTERNATIVES:** There are numerous options on the streets of Evanston. Armed with the Evanston Bikeways map, you can find your way south toward Chicago. One specific option is at 1.1 miles, go right (west) on Lincoln Street [instead of the recommended left (east)] to Hartrey Street. Left to Payne, left; cross the river to Ashland Avenue, right to Asbury, right (south) into Chicago.

**OTHER INFORMATION:** The Evanston Bikeways Map is distributed by Evanston bike shops, the Evanston Police Department and the Evanston Civic Center. The City of Evanston City Clerk sent a map by mail. The telephone number is (847) 328-2100.

**PARKING:** Good multiday parking on the Northwestern University Campus on the weekends. Otherwise, you have a lot of street parking, but with restrictions.

**SIDE TRIPS:** With an Evanston Bikeways Map, you will find there are a number of side trips through the city streets of Evanston.

**DIRECTIONS (Mile marker/**Description):
**0.0** Isabella Street and Poplar Drive. East on Isabella (at boundary between Wilmette and Evanston.

**0.5** Past the athletic fields of Northwestern University.

**0.7** Asbury Avenue, right (south); just before the railroad tracks.

**1.0** Cross Central Avenue.

**1.1** Lincoln Street, left (east); cross bridge over Evanston River. (Some call it Evanston Sewage Canal.)

**1.4** Cross Ridge Avenue toward Northwestern University.

**1.8** Cross Sheridan Road and go into Northwestern University campus.

**1.9** Bear right (south) on the campus road.

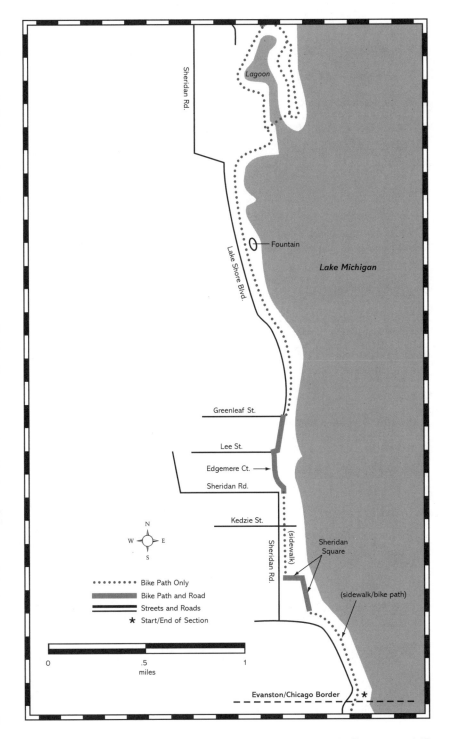

Sheridan Rd.

Lagoon

Lake Shore Blvd.

Fountain

*Lake Michigan*

Greenleaf St.

Lee St.

Edgemere Ct. →

Sheridan Rd.

Kedzie St.

N
W ✦ E
S

Sheridan Rd.

(sidewalk)

Sheridan
Square

(sidewalk/bike path)

● ● ● ● ● ● Bike Path Only
▬▬▬▬▬ Bike Path and Road
▬▬▬▬▬ Streets and Roads
★ Start/End of Section

0          .5          1
miles

Evanston/Chicago Border          ★

**13. Evanston** 147

**2.0** Henry Crown Sports Center.

**2.1** Left (east) at stop sign for 1 block on a campus road.

**2.2** Bike path, right (south). The path is on the east side of campus road.

**2.3** Two options equidistant.

> **OPTION A:** Right (south) on campus side of the lagoon.
>
> **OPTION B:** Straight (east) to the peninsula, then right (south). There are two paths on the peninsula: a) along the lagoon; b) along the lake (views of Chicago Loop). These merge and go west and over the foot bridge.

**2.8** The two paths rejoin. One from the east and one from the west. Turn south on the bike path at the T junction. The best view yet of the Chicago Loop.

**2.9** Bike path turns right (west).

**3.0** Bear left along the beach.

**3.1** Enter the park along the beach, out of campus on the bike path, south.

**3.4** Fountain in pond in the City of Evanston Park.

**3.8** Bear left (south) on the bike path. Good views.

**4.0** Bathrooms and water fountain.

**4.1** Off path onto Lake Shore Boulevard (parallel); south at Greenleaf Street for 1 block.

**4.2** Edgemere Court, quick right, then left (south). Disregard the "Dead End" sign; south for 1 block.

**4.3** Then onto sidewalk on left and through the fence onto a sidewalk next to Sheridan Road (busy road). Stay on sidewalk south.

**4.7** Sheridan Square, left (east); 1 block.

**4.7** Street swings right (south) one way going south. Also crushed stone path on the east side of the road.

**4.9** Sheridan Road, bear left on paved, narrow bike path/sidewalk adjacent to Sheridan Road; first east, then south.

**5.3** Bear west on the sidewalk/bike path. Enter Chicago. Eastlake Terrace, left (south).

# 16. Chicago Street Connection

## 3.4 miles

*A marked, recommended bike route from the lakefront in Evanston to the beginning of the Lake Front Bike Path. All on city streets. Serious gaps in signage for the bike route.*

**ROUTE:** This section starts at the Evanston/Chicago boundary on the sidewalk on the east side of Sheridan Road. The whole route is on city streets and takes you to the start of the Lake Front Bike Path.

**SURFACE:** City streets. Sometimes rough, sometimes smooth.

**TRAFFIC:** Moderate traffic except on major streets. Parked cars on both sides of the street. The one-way streets are narrow, but traffic is moderate and has room to pass you.

**POINTS OF INTEREST:** Urban residential area and shopping districts.

**FACILITIES:** Many restaurants and stores on Granville Avenue and Devon Avenue.

**SIDE LIGHTS:** The Heartland Cafe at Lunt and Glenwood has good food (including breakfast) and the counterculture attitude of the '60s and Berkeley.

**ALTERNATIVES:** Sheridan Road would be the most direct, but the traffic is intense and the lanes are narrow. Just south of Evanston it is illegal to bicycle on Sheridan Road.

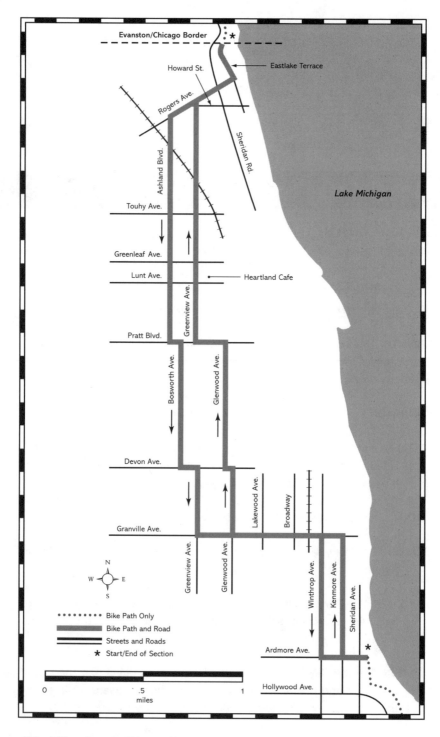

Evanston/Chicago Border

✳

Howard St.

Eastlake Terrace

Rogers Ave.

Sheridan Rd.

Lake Michigan

Ashland Blvd.

Touhy Ave.

Greenleaf Ave.

Lunt Ave.

Heartland Cafe

Greenview Ave.

Pratt Blvd.

Bosworth Ave.

Glenwood Ave.

Devon Ave.

Granville Ave.

Lakewood Ave.

Broadway

Greenview Ave.

Glenwood Ave.

Winthrop Ave.

Kenmore Ave.

Sheridan Ave.

N
W ─✧─ E
S

········· Bike Path Only
▬▬▬▬ Bike Path and Road
───── Streets and Roads
✳ Start/End of Section

Ardmore Ave.

✳

0            .5            1
miles

Hollywood Ave.

**OTHER INFORMATION:** My only recommendation is a good street map of Chicago. These can be obtained at any gas station in Chicago.

**PARKING:** Parking on this route section would be on the street, hard to find and not always secure, especially for multiple days.

**SIDE TRIPS:** Limitless on Chicago streets but none of any real interest on a bike.

**DIRECTIONS (Mile marker/**Description):

**0.0** Enter Chicago on sidewalk/bike path on east side of Sheridan Road. Leaving Evanston on lakefront.

**0.0** Eastlake Terrace, left (south). Signs for the bike route; one way south, 1 block.

**0.1** Rogers Avenue, right (west) 1 block (7656N).

**0.2** Cross Sheridan Road, continue west on Rogers Avenue.

**0.4** Ashland Boulevard, left (south); Lake Front Bike Route; two-way street, moderate traffic.

**0.5** Under the EL Tracks.

**0.8** Cross Touhy Avenue.

**1.0** Cross Greenleaf Avenue.

**1.1** Cross Lunt Avenue (7000 N). The Heartland Cafe is to the east off the bike route (2 blocks).

**1.3** Pratt Boulevard, left (east) 150 feet. Bosworth, right (south) 1 way south.

**1.9** Devon Avenue, left (east). Pratt Boulevard ends. No signs.

**1.9** Immediately right (south) on Greenview Avenue; 2-way street, narrow.

**2.2** Granville Avenue, left (east), narrow 2-way.

**2.6** Cross Broadway.

**2.7** Winthrop Avenue, right (south); 1-way street, south.

**3.2** Ardmore Avenue, left (east); 1-way street, narrow. There is a bike lane.

**3.3** Cross Sheridan Road.

**3.4** To lakefront, bear right (south) on the Chicago Lake Front Bike Path.

# 17. Lake Front Bike Path

## *9.1 miles*

*The best, most dramatic urban bike path in America. The whole path stretches 18.5 miles from Hollywood Avenue (5700 N) to 71st Street on the south side. The course is marked and measured and runs through five lakefront parks.*

**ROUTE:** Start at Hollywood Avenue and end at Buckingham Fountain (east of the Loop). The path runs east of Lake Shore Drive from beginning to end in a north/south direction. At times the path meanders through the parks. There are entrances and exits at all the major streets.

**SURFACE:** Paved. The path is sometimes new, smooth, blacktop and sometimes rougher reconverted city sidewalks.

**TRAFFIC:** No car traffic but bike, rollerblade, jogger and walker traffic can be heavy, especially around Ohio Street and Oak Street beaches and on weekends.

**POINTS OF INTEREST:** Chicago's skyline on the west and the Lake Michigan lakefront on the east. Navy Pier, Buckingham Fountain, Lincoln Park, Grant Park and Montrose Harbor.

**FACILITIES:** Water fountains at intervals. Restrooms in parks. Occasional food stands and at 2.8 miles, the Waveland Cafe.

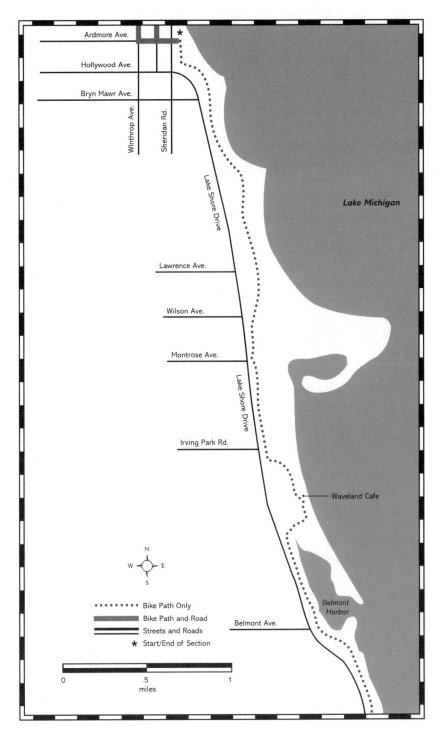

Ardmore Ave.

Hollywood Ave.

Bryn Mawr Ave.

Winthrop Ave.

Sheridan Rd.

Lake Shore Drive

Lake Michigan

Lawrence Ave.

Wilson Ave.

Montrose Ave.

Lake Shore Drive

Irving Park Rd.

Waveland Cafe

N
W — E
S

•••••••• Bike Path Only

Bike Path and Road

Streets and Roads

★ Start/End of Section

Belmont Harbor

Belmont Ave.

0          .5          1
        miles

**17. Lake Front Bike Path   153**

**SIDE LIGHTS:** Chicago comes to play on the lakefront. You will pass dog beaches, baseball diamonds, basketball courts, soccer fields, volleyball on the beach, touch football and beach action.

**ALTERNATIVES:** City streets on the west side of Lake Shore Drive are not a good alternative.

**OTHER INFORMATION:** The Chicago Park District offers free maps of the full Lake Front Bike Way. Contact:

Chicago Park District
Lakefront Region Office
South Shore Cultural Center
7059 South Shore Drive
Chicago, Illinois 60649
(312) 747-2474

Additional information can be obtained from the Chicagoland Bicycle Federation, (312) 427-3325 (42-PEDAL)

**PARKING:** Multiday parking in parks along the lake is risky. Break-ins are fairly common. You're better off in secured paid lots nearby. Only street parking near the north end of the bike path.

**SIDE TRIPS:** Navy Pier Path. Restaurants, bars, etc. 1.3 miles round trip to end through heavy pedestrian traffic. Most likely you will have to walk your bike part of the way. There are no signs that say you can't ride your bike. The road on the north side of the Pier is for auto traffic.

**DIRECTIONS (Mile marker/**Description):

**0.0** Lake Front Bike Path starts at Ardmore Avenue, one block east of Sheridan Road.

**1.4** Lawrence Avenue.

**1.6** Wilson Avenue. Restrooms and water fountain available along the path at intervals.

**1.9** Montrose Avenue.

**2.1** Onto converted sidewalk, cement, along Lake Shore Drive.

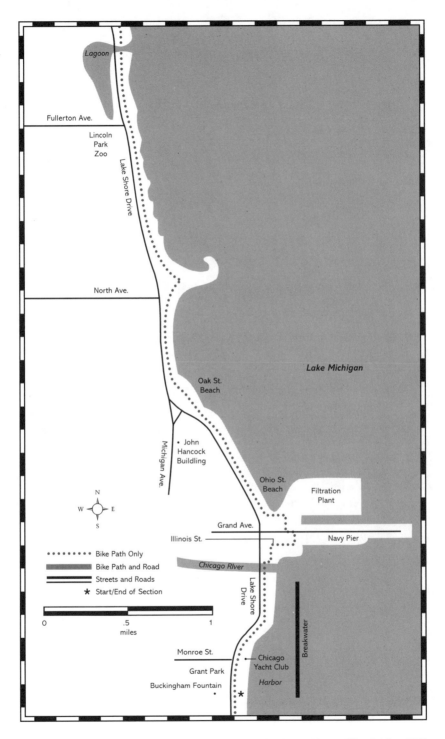

Lagoon

Fullerton Ave.

Lincoln
Park
Zoo

Lake Shore Drive

North Ave.

*Lake Michigan*

Oak St.
Beach

Michigan Ave.

• John
Hancock
Buildimg

Ohio St.
Beach

Filtration
Plant

Grand Ave.

Illinois St.

Navy Pier

•••••• Bike Path Only

Bike Path and Road

Streets and Roads

★ Start/End of Section

*Chicago River*

Lake Shore Drive

N
W   E
S

0    .5    1
miles

Breakwater

Monroe St.

Chicago
Yacht Club

Grant Park

*Harbor*

Buckingham Fountain •

★

**17. Lake Front Bike Path**   155

**2.5** Irving Park Road.

**2.8** Waveland Cafe; cute place for snacks and drinks, breakfast, etc.

**3.3** Belmont Harbor.

**3.7** Belmont Avenue, rough pavement.

**3.8** End of Belmont Harbor.

**4.4** Out onto breakwater; great views.

**4.8** Fullerton Avenue.

**5.8** North Avenue.

**6.0** Vista of Loop.

**6.6** Opposite the start of Michigan Avenue; the Miracle Mile.

**6.9** Along lake. On wavy days you might be riding in some surf.

**7.5** Path swings east into the park; approaching Navy Pier.

**7.7** East on Grand Avenue toward Navy Pier on the lakefront path.

**7.8** Bear right (west) on bike path.

**7.9** Illinois Street, left (south) along Lake Shore Drive over bridge over Chicago River.

**8.2** Off bridge onto path.

**8.7** Monroe Street; Chicago Yacht Club.

**9.1** Opposite Buckingham Fountain on Lake Front Bike Path. You are east of the Chicago Loop.

# 18. Excursion

## *8.5 miles*

*You start on the Lake Front Bike Path opposite Buckingham Fountain. This is the most spectacular urban bike path in America. The path runs east of Lake Shore Drive from beginning to end. Our route starts in front of the Loop. The whole path stretches 18.5 miles from Hollywood Avenue (5100 N) to 71st Street on the south. The course is measured and marked and runs through Grant Park, Burnham Park and Jackson Park.*

**ROUTE:** The route is along Lake Michigan to the south of the Loop. The path always runs east of Lake Shore Drive. In the past there have been some safety concerns, but there seems to be more police protection now.

**SURFACE:** The whole bike path is paved. The surface is occasionally a little rough farther south.

**TRAFFIC:** From Buckingham Fountain to McCormick Place the path can be very crowded with bikers and walkers. Especially around the Shedd Aquarium on weekends, the foot traffic will slow you down. After McCormick Place the bike traffic is light.

**POINTS OF INTEREST:** The fabulous views of the Chicago skyline. Buckingham Fountain, Field Museum, Shedd Aquarium, Adler Planetarium, McCormick Place, Promontory Point, Museum of

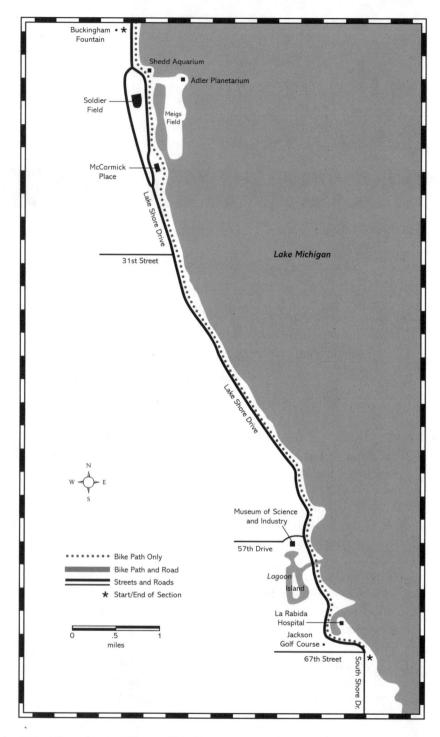

Buckingham • ✱
Fountain

Shedd Aquarium

Adler Planetarium

Soldier
Field

Meigs
Field

McCormick
Place

Lake Shore Drive

31st Street

Lake Michigan

Lake Shore Drive

N
W ✦ E
S

Museum of Science
and Industry

57th Drive

•••••••• Bike Path Only
▬▬▬▬ Bike Path and Road
▬▬▬▬ Streets and Roads
✱ Start/End of Section

Lagoon
Island

La Rabida
Hospital

Jackson
Golf Course •

0    .5    1
miles

67th Street

South Shore Dr.

✱

Science and Industry and the 59th Street Beach and Harbor.

**FACILITIES:** There are water fountains and bathrooms along the path. There are temporary snack bars set up along the lakefront around the Shedd Aquarium. South of McCormick Place, there is no food available on the path.

**SIDE LIGHTS:** Soldier Field, home of DA BEARS. Off the path, out on the peninsula on which the Adler Planetarium is located, is a statue of Nicolaus Copernicus, the noted Polish astronomer. While you pass McCormick Place you realize its size. (One million square feet.)

**ALTERNATIVES:** At times there are alternative paths through the parks and along the lake. In the very beginning you can ride your bike along the breakwater at the harbor's edge.

**OTHER INFORMATION:** For information on the Chicago Park District Bike Way or to order Bike Way maps, contact the Chicago Park District's Lakefront Region Office at the South Shore Cultural Center, 7059 South Shore Drive, Chicago, Illinois 60649. (312) 747-2474.

**PARKING:** Underground parking is available in Grant Park at Monroe and Columbus and along Michigan Avenue. Also, there are metered spots at most beach and park locations, although security is a concern.

**SIDE TRIPS:** You can ride out on the Adler Planetarium peninsula. Round trip is .5 miles. The views are more spectacular.

**DIRECTIONS (Mile marker/**Description):

**0.0** Lake Front Bike Path across from Buckingham Fountain. Go south.

**0.6** Shedd Aquarium and Adler Planetarium.

**1.0** Soldier Field.

**1.7** McCormick Place. Path goes behind (lake side) McCormick Place.

**6.6** 57th Drive, across from the Museum of Science and Industry.

**8.1** Pass Rabida Children's Hospital. Beautiful area.

**8.5** 67th Street, end of bike path. Jackson Golf Course. Lake Shore Drive ends and becomes South Shore Drive.